The defense of Moscow

D1563174

Geoffrey Jukes
The defence

of Moscow

BB

Editor-in-Chief: Barrie Pitt
Art Director: Peter Dunbar

Military Consultant: Sir Basil Liddell Hart
Picture Editor: Robert Hunt

Executive Editor: David Mason
Designer: Sarah Kingham
Special Drawings: John Batchelor
Cartographer: Richard Natkiel
Cover: Denis Piper
Research Assistant: Yvonne Marsh

Copyright © 1970 by Geoffrey Jukes

SBN 345-01943-1-100

First printing: June 1970
Printed in United States of America

Ballantine Books Inc.
101 Fifth Avenue New York NY 10003

Contents

Hitler's first defeat

Introduction by General Hasso von Manteuffel

In his Directive No 21 of 18th December 1940, Hitler established the aim of the Barbarossa Campaign: 'The Soviet Union is to be crushed in one *swift* campaign before the war ends with England, and the opening attacks will prepare the way for the occupation of the vital communications and armament centre, Moscow'. In subsequent discussions of military operations however, it became increasingly apparent that a discrepancy existed between the thinking of Hitler and his advisors in the High Command of the Armed Forces (OKW) on the one hand, and that of the German Army High Command (OKH) on the other. Hitler was striving to put into practice the theories of *Mein Kampf* in that he was preoccupied with political and ideological factors as well as military economics. This duality in the minds of Hitler and his closest aides hindered the campaign from the early stages of the attack on the Soviet Union (22nd June 1941) and in the months that followed, right up to the gates of Moscow. Thus both in planning and in execution, Hitler and the OKH followed parallel but separate courses. Furthermore, when the opening attack was postponed by four of five weeks as a result of the Balkan campaign, it should have led to confinement of operations to a narrower area with concentration on one target.

Army Group Centre which had dealt heavy blows against the enemy forces in a series of extensive encircling operations was to have attacked Moscow via Minsk-Smolensk-Vyazma but it was unable to break the enemy's resistance. The swift advances of Panzer columns which in past campaigns had been the prelude to speedy victory, did not have the same effect in the East. In the vast open spaces, isolated armoured units on the move could not close in without waiting for infantry units to be brought forward. Because of this, large sections of the enemy were able to break through and evaded pursuit by the German forces once they reached the extensive areas of forest and marsh. Hitler was aware of the problem when he issued his Directive No 33 on 19th July 1941. In it he dismissed Moscow as the main objective of Army Group Centre and ordered the German forces to be divided: strong units of Army Group Centre were diverted southwards to join forces with Army Group South in the move on Kiev in order to deny the enemy an eastward retreat. Kiev fell into German hands on 19th September 1941, though the battle continued until 26th September. This 'involuntary battle' had no decisive effect. On the contrary it rendered the Panzer units immobile and caused a considerable loss of time; the objective of defeating the Soviet Union in one swift campaign was in vain. Once the attack on Moscow had been resumed on 2nd October, and once Bryansk and Vyazma had been taken on 6th and 7th October, Army Group Centre succeeded in breaking through into the Moscow defensive positions. By mid-October, the first winter snows had turned to freezing mud, which caught the German forces by surprise. They were unprepared for it and were inadequately equipped; this was one setback which had not been anticipated. At the end of November the German positions were as follows: the 3rd Panzer Division was at Klin on the Kalinin-Moscow road, and the advance units of the 7th Panzer Division were holding a bridgehead east of the Volga-Moscow Canal at Yakhroma, approximately thirty-five kilometres from Moscow; to the south, the 2nd Panzer Division was fighting for Tula south of the city; the 4th Division was engaged in a frontal assault forty kilometres from the city; attacked from the front and the flank, the German forces could advance no further. Since 22nd June 1941 they had been constantly engaged in action and were now low in morale and physical strength. Behind the German front there were no reserves to fill the huge gaps which left exposed some thousand kilometres of battle line. Not once had the Red Army used its full force to bring the German attack to a standstill, and now the Soviets saw that their hour had come. From this point on neither Hitler nor orders from the OKW dictated further events on the battlefield – only the real enemy: Zhukov. In the coming weeks and months the German army experienced how much the Red Army had learnt while halting their attack, both on the tactical and operational levels.

Seen in the broader context of the Second World War, failure to defeat the Soviet Union in four to five months signalled the end of the 'Blitzkrieg'.

From a political, economical and military point of view Hitler had underestimated the Soviet Union. In 1939 he had considered it 'a statesman-like achievement' that Germany had only to fight on one front but now the war on two fronts had become a reality as Germany had experienced once before in 1914–1918. It was apparent that Hitler's allies were disillusioned and in the occupied areas resistance to the occupying forces mounted. Turkey, which Hitler would like to have seen participate in 'his war' continued to wait on the sidelines. While the Allied resistance to Hitler received considerable uplift, England in particular found the breathing space that she so much needed to advance her military preparations and develop her alliances. The Soviet Union could rely on the Western Powers and turn its full weight against Germany and since 7th December 1941 when Japan attacked Pearl Harbor the ports of the great arsenal of democracy were open to the Soviet Union's leaders.

The battle before Moscow in the winter of 1941–1942 is rightly considered as one of the decisive battles of the Second World War. It was the last and belated act in the German design to defeat Russia. Whatever Hitler undertook from this time on could only delay his ultimate downfall.

The author of the survey that follows, Geoffrey Jukes, has become known through his books, *Stalingrad: the turning point* (Battle Book 3) and *Kursk: the clash of armour* (Battle Book 7). Possessing a thorough knowledge of the Wehrmacht and the Red Army he has built up an authentic picture of the battle before Moscow, retaining a high degree of objectivity combined with vigour and colour. This book is a worthy successor to his previous works. In my capacity as a troop-commander and witness of the beginning of the German campaign up to the successful push across the Volga-Moscow Canal and the final retreat, I am able to confirm the accuracy of the narrative.

The rise of Marshal Zhukov

If the Battle of Britain was the first occasion in the Second World War where Germany's military limitations were prominently displayed, the Battle of Moscow was the second. But otherwise there is little ground for comparison between the two battles. In the first case, the opposing spearheads, the Royal Air Force's Fighter Command, and *Luftflotten* 2, 3 and 5, consisted of air crews committed to battle in numbers seldom exceeding 1,000 on the German side, except at moments of maximum pressure, and never reaching that figure on the British side. It was a battle between technology-intensive forces, whose outcome owed much to scientific factors, such as the British possession of radar, and Germany's most outstanding weapon – its armoured forces – could not take part.

The Battle of Moscow, on the other hand, was a clash of titans, with more than a million troops engaged on each side. It was the first of several such clashes on the Eastern Front, one in which the Panzer forces, the pride of the German Army, met head on a Red Army already apparently bled to death in months of exhausting and fruitless defence, clutched confidently at the supreme prize, the capital of the world's only Communist state, saw that prize slip from their grasp, and were then forced into a retreat which almost became a rout. The Red Army's recovery, after almost all the regular forces with which it began the war had been swallowed up (there were nearly 3,500,000 Soviet troops in German prisoner of war camps by December 1941) was a remarkable feat, to which the entire country contributed in one way or another. But the direction of the defence, conducted as it had to be by a mixture of *ad hoc* units, remnants of beaten armies, hastily mobilised reserve divisions and almost totally untrained People's Militia, was primarily the work of one man. So was the selection of the precise moment at which to launch the reserves, which included almost the last of the peacetime cadre forces, the Siberian divisions of the Far Eastern Army, against German forces whose offensive impetus had petered out, but which had not yet dug in for a defensive fight. That man was the Commander of the Soviet Western Front (Army Group), General of the Army, later Marshal of the Soviet Union, Georgy Konstantinovich Zhukov.

Zhukov was born in 1896 in the village of Strelkovka of the then Kaluga Governorate southwest of Moscow. The Zhukov family, like that of many other successful Red Army generals, was exceedingly poor, and his father, a cobbler by trade, spent much time away from home in search of work. However, unlike many of his contemporaries, the young Zhukov was able to attend school, where he did well, until at the age of ten he was withdrawn to begin earning his living. In 1907 he was apprenticed to one of his mother's brothers to learn the trade of a furrier and tanner in Moscow, where he was able to continue his education at evening classes. In August 1915, because of the Russian Army's immense losses in manpower in the battles of the First World War, he was called up ahead of time into the 189th Reserve Infantry Battalion. On completion of training he was transferred to the cavalry, to the 10th Regiment of the Novgorod Dragoons, where he became a 'vice-under-officer' (roughly equivalent to a sergeant) and was wounded in action, twice receiving the high Tsarist award for valour, the Cross of St George.

Shortly after his return from hospital the February revolution of 1917 broke out. As was happening generally in the army, his squadron appointed a soldiers' committee, of which he was elected chairman and delegate to the Regimental Soviet (Council), which

Stalin's greatest general: Zhukov, the man who defeated 'Barbarossa' before the gates of Moscow

**Swashbuckling relic of the Civil War:
Marshal SM Budenny**

in March voted to support Lenin's Bolshevik Party. This act split the regiment into three hostile factions, some supporting the Bolsheviks, some the Provisional Government, which wished to continue the war, and some the Ukrainian Nationalists, who favoured Ukrainian independence. The pro-Bolshevik faction was in a decided minority, and Zhukov was forced to go into hiding for several weeks, before making his way secretly back to Moscow, where he arrived at the end of November 1917. By then the Bolsheviks had seized power in Petrograd (then the capital, and now named Leningrad), and a civil war, which was to last until 1922, had broken out.

Zhukov, who had by then linked his fortunes firmly to those of the Communist Party, decided to volunteer for the Red Guards, the nucleus of the army which the revolutionary government was raising, but before he could do so he was stricken by typhus, and not until six months later was he able to give effect to his intentions by enrolling as a private in the 1st Moscow Cavalry Division. The Red Army was exceedingly short of trained officers, as most of the officer corps had joined the White armies, and a motivated and experienced non-

commissioned officer from a crack regiment of the Imperial Army could expect to advance rapidly. By the end of the civil war Zhukov was commanding a squadron in the First Cavalry Army (whose commander, another ex-Imperial Army cavalry NCO, Semyon Mikhailovich Budenny, he was to supersede in charge of the defence of Moscow in 1941), and had decided to make the Army his career. The First Cavalry Army was the pride of the new state's armed forces, and many of the most outstanding Soviet generals were to come from its junior officer cadre. But perhaps the most important influence on his future career was that later to be exercised by Zhukov's brigade commander, Semyon Konstantinovich Timoshenko, because eighteen years later Timoshenko, by then a marshal and People's Commissar for Defence, elevated his younger colleague to the post of his principal assistant, as Chief of the General Staff.

Between the wars, Zhukov, already marked out as one of the Red Army's most promising younger professionals, had switched from cavalry to armour, had espoused the modern theories of armoured warfare which the Germans were pursuing and which the Chief of the Soviet General Staff, the brilliant Marshal Tukhachevsky, was actively propagating. However, he had not become sufficiently prominent to attract the attention of the secret police to himself when Stalin in 1938 embarked on his disastrous blood purge of the officer corps, and this was to provide him with his first opportunity to shine as commander of a large force in battle. Like many officers who were classified as 'reliable' and therefore survived the purge, he found himself promoted rapidly into posts vacated by senior officers who 'disappeared' in the terrible years of 1938-39. In July 1939 he was appointed to command the Soviet and Mongolian forces fighting a Japanese army of 75,000 men which had invaded the Mongolian People's Republic from

Timoshenko: victor of Finland, later to suffer repeated defeats

China. On 20th August 1939 he counter-attacked the Japanese, and by 31st August had driven them (or what was left of them, for 41,000 were killed, wounded or captured) back in a complete rout into China. This achievement subsequently played an important role in the Japanese decision not to attack the Soviet Union in 1941, thus making it possible for Stalin to transfer most of his Siberian divisions to the west; but it attracted little attention in a Europe which was preoccupied with the opening of the Second World War. The news from Mongolia was crowded out of the newspapers of 1st and 2nd September 1939 by the German invasion of Poland and the British and French ultimata, so Europe was to form its opinions of the Red Army and its leaders by their disastrous performance in the war against Finland three months later. Only the Japanese were to rate Soviet military power as formidable. Nevertheless, Zhukov's success led to his first meeting with Stalin, and the beginning of a relationship which developed rapidly and gave Zhukov greater influence over military decision-making than any other soldier was able to achieve.

First he was appointed deputy to his old chief, Timoshenko, at the head-quarters of the Ukrainian Military District, and when Timoshenko was despatched to the north in January 1940 to take command in the war against Finland, accompanied him as Chief of Staff. Between them they brought that disastrously mishandled campaign to a successful conclusion, and Stalin then appointed Timoshenko People's Commissar for Defence, with the task of restoring military effectiveness to the Red Army. Timoshenko appointed Zhukov to the post he had previously held himself, now renamed the 'Kiev Special Military District', and one of the most important field commands, because of its long border with German-occupied Poland. While here he made his first public speech, on 11th December 1940, stressing the need for emphasis on military qualities (implicitly in contrast to the quality of loyalty to the Party leadership) attacking some of the older members of the High Command, many of whom were classic and disastrous examples of promotion attained by loyalty to Stalin rather than by military talent, and hinting at the need to prepare for war against Germany. This was, perhaps, the most dangerous utterance of all, since it implied that the German-Soviet Alliance of 1939 could not rule out such a possibility, and therefore suggested that Stalin could be hoodwinked. Neither Zhukov nor any Soviet historian has explained why he made this speech, nor why, having made it, he was not punished: many of his colleagues had been penalised for less. Nevertheless, the philosophy which he then expressed, stressing the need for military operations to be in the hands of trusted professionals, not subjected to the division of control inherent in the old system of political overseers, was to remain characteristic of him, and to find concrete expression when he became Minister of Defence after Stalin's death.

Whatever the reasons for his public manifestation of dissent from certain aspects of government policy, he

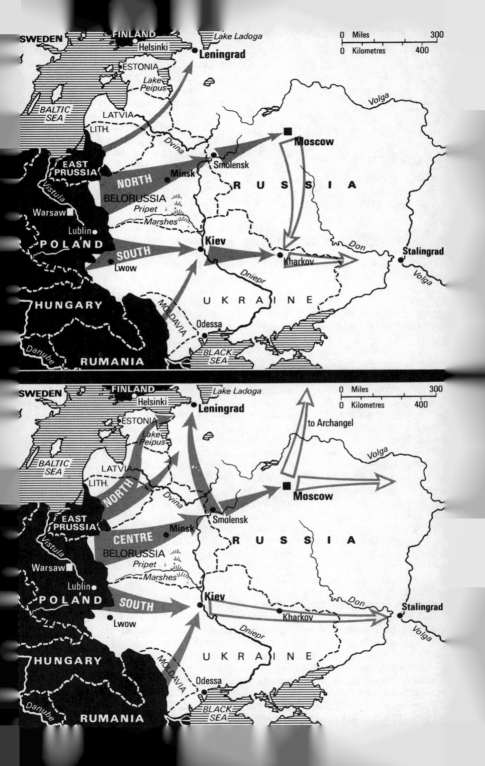

Above left: Marcks Plan: heavy thrusts towards Moscow and Kiev, with the Baltic and Black Sea flanks left to much lighter forces. *Left:* OKH Plan: Leningrad becomes a third primary objective, while the Moscow thrust is strengthened at the expense of the drive on Kiev. *Above:* Hitler's variant, 'Barbarossa': the capture of Leningrad is stipulated as essential before the subsequent – and conclusive – drive on Moscow

Above: Russia's generalissimo, Stalin, whose drastic purges of the army in the late 1930s decimated the Red Army's officer corps. *Far right:* Marshal BM Shaposhnikov, who replaced Zhukov as Chief of the Red Army's General Staff

suffered no apparent ill-effects from it. Indeed, a mere two months later, in January 1941, he was to receive yet another promotion. The occasion was a conference of high-level commanders in Moscow, at which a series of papers were delivered on problems of modern warfare, and a war game was held, assuming a German attack. Zhukov's part both in the conference and in the war game was a prominent one. At the end of the proceedings, Stalin summoned the senior officers to meet at two hours' notice, and ordered the Chief of General Staff, General Meretskov, to report on the exercise. Meretskov, inadequately briefed at such short notice, delivered an unsatisfactory report, as anyone might in his place. Stalin waited until he had finished, then turned to Zhukov. 'Comrade Timoshenko has asked that Comrade Zhukov be appointed Chief of the General Staff. Are you all in favour?' No one dared object, so on 14th January 1941 Zhukov ascended to the second highest post in the Red Army, at the age of forty-four, and over the heads of many who may well have felt they had a better claim.

In his new post, his main duty was to assist his old patron Timoshenko in removing the faults shown up by the Finnish war, and preparing the Red Army to fight the war with Germany which more and more began to appear inevitable. But the magnitude of the task, and Stalin's belief that he could postpone the confrontation at least until 1942, meant that no major benefits could be expected from the modernisation programme for at least a year. And Hitler was to attack in six months and eight days from the date of Zhukov's appointment. When the attack came, Timoshenko and Zhukov found their forces melting away into German prison camps, their air forces destroyed on the ground, and Stalin either issuing no orders at all, which paralysed the Soviet war machine because the purges had taught everyone that the exercise of initiative was dangerous, or ordering the troops to stand fast, when military prudence dictated that they trade space for time, by withdrawing to avoid encirclement. At Kiev an entire army group was annihilated because Stalin would not permit the city to be given up; the Germans claimed 665,000 prisoners. The Soviets angrily deny this but admit to losses of 527,000 in two months, while glossing over the fate of at least ten reserve divisions despatched to the Ukraine after the outbreak of hostilities, and probably also lost, adding about 100,000 to the total. In all the months from 22nd June to the beginning of the German assault on Moscow on 30th September, the only battle which can be claimed as a victory was Zhukov's operation at Yelnya in August and September, where the Germans were expelled from the town, although they escaped his attempt at encirclement by a narrow margin. All else was either utter failure or expensive delaying action, buying time with blood, and with its usefulness assessable only in the

General IS Konev, Zhukov's deputy as commander of Western Front during the Moscow fighting

future when the other battles, for which it bought the time, had been fought.

By the beginning of the autumn Timoshenko and Zhukov had long ceased to hold sedentary posts in the Ministry of Defence. Stalin had assumed the role of Commander-in-Chief, and Marshal Shaposhnikov, a former Imperial Army Colonel, one of the few relatively senior Tsarist officers to espouse the communist cause, had taken over the General Staff. A General Headquarters (STAVKA) had been set up, and the erstwhile People's Commissar and his deputy, as members of it, were despatched now hither, now thither, to stabilise the fast-melting front. It was in this capacity as a trouble-shooter that Zhukov brought the Panzers grinding to a temporary halt at Yelnya, when he deployed the six armies of his Reserve Front forward to fight the twenty-six day battle of the Yelnya Salient and halt Army

Hitler to assess Army Group North's effort as 'a failure', and soon its armour, Colonel-General Hoeppner's Panzer Group 4 was to begin moving southwards to take part in the offensive against Moscow. But they could have played only a minor part in the taking of Leningrad, as cities are the worst operating terrain for mobile forces. Occupying the city would have been a task for the infantry divisions, and had there been manifest signs of weakness in the defence, they would have pressed forward to the target which Hitler persistently rated above Moscow for its strategic position and its symbolic importance as the cradle of the Communist revolution. Subsequently the city was to withstand a 900 day siege in which, though countless thousands of its citizens died of starvation and hunger, it was never again as close to capture as it had been in the days immediately before Zhukov's arrival.

From Leningrad Zhukov was summoned to Moscow by Stalin on 6th October, to find a situation of the utmost peril. In effect the defences of three army groups (Western, Reserve and Bryansk Fronts) had fallen apart under the German onslaught, the Panzer columns had broken through, and there was almost nothing between them and the capital. How Zhukov coped with the situation is described in his own words later in this book. Suffice it here to say that he turned the tables and inflicted on the Germans their first major defeat on land of the entire war, so shattering Hitler's confidence in his generals that he dismissed the Commander-in-Chief of the Army, the three Army Group Commanders, and thirty-one other generals. German losses in men, material and morale were no less significant, in that never again throughout the war was Germany in a position to mount an offensive on more than one strategic axis at a time.

Group Centre's advance on Moscow. On 10th September Stalin summoned Zhukov to Moscow. Leningrad was under siege by Army Group North, and its fall appeared imminent. Zhukov was ordered to take charge there, and he arrived on 12th September. In three days of savage energy he restored order to the flagging defenders, dismissing large numbers of senior officers, sending some to the firing squad for unauthorised retreats, and bringing Army Group North to a halt. Though he did not know it at the time, his fierce energy caused

Hitler turns against Russia

In September 1939 the new-model German army swept into Poland behind spearheads of tanks and motorised infantry, and under a screen of dive-bombers. The Poles, inadequately equipped and led for a modern war, were the unwilling subjects for the first full-scale tests of the theories of armoured warfare, first advanced in the 1920s by British thinkers such as Liddell Hart, but enthusiastically espoused only by a relatively small number of officers of defeated Germany's 100,000 man Reichswehr. The leading personality among these, Heinz Guderian, had succeeded in overcoming the opposition of conservatively-minded superiors, in building up and testing a model formation centred around the tank and the lorry-borne infantryman, and finally in capturing Hitler's enthusiasm and support for the new concept. Other armies, too, had experimented with the ideas of the British theorists, but for a variety of reasons the philosophy of mobility had failed to take a hold. As a result the tank continued in the main to be regarded as an infantry support weapon, the unit of tactical mobility to be the foot soldier, marching at about three-and-a-half miles per hour and advancing in combat, with due regard to the safety of his flanks, at much less than that. Only in the new Wehrmacht of the late 1930s were there sizable forces which could move at the pace of a tank, about twenty miles per hour, in which the infantry were lorry-borne, to bring their speed up to that of the tanks', rather than vice-versa, and in which it was a matter of principle to move ahead fast with only such regard for flank protection as a minimal prudence dictated.

The six-fold increase in tactical

mobility thus achieved was to be utilised to penetrate the line formations of a conventional army, thus forcing it into encirclement between the mobile forces behind it, and the masses of conventional infantry in front of it. If it chose to avoid encirclement by withdrawal, it would be harried by the mobile forces, so that it would be unable to stabilise its positions, and retreat would be turned into rout, aided by the constant activity of the dive-bombers overhead.

Against Poland the revolutionary concept of warfare worked brilliantly, and in less than three weeks the campaign was in all essentials concluded. Eight months later, in May 1940, Guderian's doctrines faced an even bigger test, when the new forces were unleashed against France, Holland and Belgium, whose armies, together with the British Expeditionary Force, outnumbered those of Germany. Six weeks of campaigning achieved the French surrender, which the Kaiser's army had sought in vain for the four years and three months of the First World War, drove the British back over the Channel, less many of their men and most of their heavy weapons, and exposed the British Isles to a threat of invasion more direct than they had experienced since 1805. The British braced themselves for an unaccustomed ordeal; there had been no successful invasion of Britain since 1066, but no power had dominated the European continent as Germany seemed to in 1940.

For a number of reasons, political and psychological as well as military, the threat failed to become reality. Hitler's view of the British was an exceedingly involved and ambivalent one. He was prepared to tolerate the continued existence of the British Empire, provided England would confirm him in his mastery of Europe, and though his Gestapo prepared bloodcurdling plans for seizure of leading figures and deportation of able-bodied males to the continent once England had been subjugated, Hitler at that

The mask of friendship: Molotov signs the 1939 non-aggression pact while Ribbentrop and Stalin look on. The pact was blown to the winds when 'Barbarossa' opened on 22nd June 1941

19

stage hoped that the British would 'see reason', realise the hopelessness of fighting on without allies, and agree to a negotiated peace which would make his conquests permanent. That he misjudged the temper of the British in adversity is a matter of history, but so is his ambivalence towards the idea of their elimination from the equations of world power.

Nevertheless, once the British had returned an unequivocal refusal to the idea of a negotiated peace, preparations for the invasion, appropriately codenamed 'Operation Sea-Lion', went ahead, and here, naturally, the strategic factors obtruded.

The key to success lay in the ability to land and supply an army across the English Channel, and consequently the attitude of the German navy was crucial. The enthusiasm of its leaders for the enterprise was tempered by their knowledge that the surface forces of the Royal Navy were considerably superior to their own in number, and could be expected to fight effectively in defence of home territory, from main bases near at hand, and with a centuries-old tradition of ultimate success. Only the new factor of air power could change the balance of forces in favour of the Kriegsmarine, and this meant recourse to the Luftwaffe, as the German navy possessed no combat air forces of its own.

At first the Luftwaffe, personified by its leader, the fat Reichsmarshall Hermann Göring, was confident that it could gain air superiority over the Royal Air Force in a matter of days. But as the days lengthened into weeks, and the weeks into months, it became clear that the British, though hard pressed at times, were clearly holding their own at the very least, that the losses they were inflicting on the Luftwaffe were greater than their own in aircraft. and very much

The Führer and the field-marshal: Hitler and von Rundstedt discuss the southern flank

greater than their losses in the really crucial factor in the Battle of Britain – aircrew, especially pilots. As July passed into August, and August into September, it became evident that air superiority, the prerequisite to 'Sea-Lion', was not to be gained in the near future, before the onset of winter storms in the Channel made supply an uncertain undertaking. The Battle of Britain had shown, for the first time since the war began, that Germany's chain of military success could be broken. Because the Luftwaffe could not prevail, Germany's strongest weapon, its hitherto invincible army, could not be brought into play, against an antagonist whose own weakened land forces could probably not have withstood it for very long if it had.

None of this however, cast any doubt upon the effectiveness of the army itself. It was the air force and navy which had proved inadequate. And there was, on the continent of Europe, another power, not subject to Hitler's will, whose continued existence meant that his domination of the continent was incomplete, whose territory was accessible over land, and towards which Hitler's attitude was entirely devoid of ambiguity. That power was the Soviet Union, ruled by the Georgian dictator Joseph Stalin.

At that time the two countries were nominally allies; indeed, it was the alliance, the Molotov-Ribbentrop Pact, signed on 25th August 1939, which had made possible the German invasion of Poland and brought about the outbreak of the war. But whatever tactical considerations might dictate, there could be no doubt of the long-term antagonism between the two dictatorships. Ever since the early days of the Nazi Party, Hitler had regarded his Communist neighbour to the east as a most deadly manifestation of the 'International Jewish conspiracy' which he blamed for Germany's misfortunes. There would be discussions over spheres of influence to be parcelled out once the

British Empire was available for dismemberment, but neither government really believed in the possibility of long-term coexistence. And it is significant of Hitler's attitudes to Great Britain on the one hand and the Soviet Union on the other, that he uttered the fatal sentence 'We must deal with Russia,' at a secret conference with senior officers of OKH (the high command of the army), on 21st July 1940. That date was a mere four weeks after the French surrender, and the Battle of Britain had just begun. The official German opening date for it, Eagle Day (13th August) was, indeed, over three weeks away.

Neither OKH, responsible for the operational planning, nor OKW, the high command of the armed forces, responsible for the allocation and movement of the necessary forces, at that time allowed their intoxicating successes of 1939 and 1940 to blind them to the difficulties inherent in this much larger enterprise. It was no secret that to follow elusive Russian armies into the vast spaces of the steppes had brought disaster to great military leaders of the past, including Napoleon, and that a prolonged campaign, which would give Russia time to mobilise its large resources of manpower, was unlikely to turn out successfully. From the beginning of the planning process it was accepted by almost all the military that the Red Army should be brought to battle as quickly and as far west as possible, preferably west of the line of the Rivers Dvina and Dnieper, but certainly west of Moscow. The campaign should begin in May 1941, i.e. after the spring thaw, which turns most of the roads (few of which are surfaced) into ribbons of mud, and should be brought to an end within seventeen weeks at the outside, i.e. before the return of the mud with the autumn rains. Intelligence on the Red Army was deficient in some respects, but it was

assumed that it could deploy 119 divisions (96 infantry and 23 cavalry) plus 28 mechanised brigades, against which Germany with 146 divisions (24 Panzer, 12 motorised and 110 infantry) would have numerical superiority.

While Generals Marcks and Feyerabend were producing operational outline plans for OKH, OKW was working on its own appreciation. The Marcks plan envisaged two main thrusts, one through Belorussia to Moscow, the other through the Ukraine to Kiev. They would operate independently, with minimal regard to their flanks, along classic Panzer warfare lines, until the northern group had captured Moscow, when it would swing southwards into the rear of the Soviet forces facing the southern group. The OKW study, on the other hand, contemplated deployment of three groups (North, Centre and South) aimed at Leningrad, Moscow and Kiev respectively, and was more conventional, in that it assumed that they would protect each other's flanks by advancing at approximately the same pace.

It has already been said that German intelligence on the Red Army was deficient in some respects. An important step was taken to remedy these deficiencies when in October 1940 it was decided to authorise air reconnaissance missions over Soviet territory, aimed at identifying military areas, barracks, airfields, and similar military targets. As the months went by these missions were extended deeper and deeper into the Soviet Union, and evaluation of the photographs taken by these forerunners of the American U-2s necessitated an upward re-evaluation of Red Army strength in the central area (from Brest to Moscow). This discovery, and the results of war games held by OKH in late November and early December 1940 reinforced General Marcks's earlier conclusion that the assault force aimed at Moscow would have to be a par-

The army and the Party: Sokolovsky, Zhukov, and I S Khoklov (left)

Above: Panzer spearhead: massed German armour punched through the Soviet front and stabbed deep into the Russian heartland. *Left:* Infantry backbone: the long, dust-blown colomns followed the tank-tracks and broke down the surrounded Russian pockets

ticularly strong one. Matters had now advanced far enough for a presentation of views to be made to Hitler, and on 5th December the Chief of General Staff of OKH, Colonel-General Halder summed up the conclusions thus far reached. His statement showed that a certain fusion of thought between OKH and OKW had taken place, in that the OKW study's advocacy of a three-pronged attack had been adopted. Halder pointed out that the

three main centres of armament production, and hence the three areas which the Red Army would have to defend if it were to be able to fight a long war, were those of Leningrad, Moscow and Kiev. These areas therefore constituted three strategic targets, and an army group should be assigned to each. The Russians could not defend these areas unless they stood and fought west of the Dvina-Dnieper line, as the Germans wanted them to. Two of the army groups would fight to the north of the Pripet marshes, and one to the south, thus placing the main weight of effort along the Leningrad and Moscow axes.

It was in Hitler's remarks on this presentation that the first indications appeared of divergence from the generally accepted military view on the prime importance of Moscow as a strategic target – a divergence which was to bedevil the conduct of operations the following summer. Hitler agreed with Halder that the central army group, operating along the Warsaw-Moscow axis, should be stronger than the others, but justified it on the grounds of a possible need to swing part of its forces northwards to assist the northern group in eliminating Soviet formations encircled in the Baltic States, rather than by the importance of its own objective.

So far the operation had had no overall codename given to it. OKH called it 'Otto', and OKW gave it no name at all. Shortly after the Halder-Hitler discussion OKW was ordered to bring together the various planning documents, and transmute them into the highest form of order, an OKW Führer Directive signed by Hitler. The Draft Directive 21, codenamed 'Fritz', was submitted to Hitler on 17th December, and emerged the next day under the more imposing codename 'Barbarossa', which evoked the memory of the mediaeval Emperor Friedrich, in an attempt to shroud a campaign of pillage and conquest in the mantle of a Crusade.

However important the change of name may be as a pointer to Hitler's state of mind, the changes of substance between the 'Fritz' draft and the 'Barbarossa' Directive are of far greater moment to the military historian. The Führer elaborated on his remarks of 5th December, by directing specifically that after Army Group Centre had destroyed the Soviet forces in Belorussia it should detach strong elements of mobile forces, to assist Army Group North in wiping out the Red Army along the Baltic. Thus he assigned to Army Group Centre a task which conflicted with the assault on Moscow which both OKW and OKH had come to view as its principal assignment. Strangely, neither OKW nor OKH registered any protest, though many German generals were later to hold this conflict of missions as the main reason why the 1941 campaign attained only one of its three objectives – Kiev.

The Directive was now elaborated further into detailed plans for its realisation. These were finalised by the end of January 1941, and presented to the Führer on 3rd February. The revised intelligence assessments had put paid to the notion that Germany would enjoy numerical superiority throughout the campaign. It was now expected that the Soviets would deploy 155 divisions (100 infantry, 25 cavalry and 30 mechanised, suspiciously rounded figures indicating that German intelligence still lacked precision) against 134 German (20 Panzer, 13 motorised and 101 infantry). However it was expected that Soviet training, equipment and leadership would be grossly inferior to that of the Germans, who would also in due course receive the assistance of an unspecified number of Roumanian divisions.

Hitler commented, on the plans, that if the Russians succeeded in disengaging to the east, and thus avoiding the battle of annihilation, the German flanks must be strengthened and the Red Army pinned down in the centre so that it could later be destroyed by concentric blows from north and south. Again the General Staff maintained a polite silence while Hitler not merely displayed his dissent from their view of the importance of the thrust at Moscow, but also raised in this casual fashion the possibility that the entire Blitzkrieg strategy might fail, that the Russians might avoid destruction west of the Dvina-Dnieper line, and withdraw to fight the prolonged war which it was the entire plan's purpose to avert. Not until the following summer did they take open issue with him on this question, and the arguments which then took place are discussed in greater detail in Chapter Three. For the moment it is enough to note that the difference of emphasis between Hitler and OKH existed as early as the end of 1940, and did not arise only late in 1941, after it became clear that not all strategic objectives could be attained, and it therefore became necessary to choose between them.

It was intended to have all the invasion forces in place by 15th May 1941, and OKH expected their concealment of their intentions would be almost impossible after mid-April, thus giving the Red Army about one month's tactical warning that war was imminent. However, contempt for their military qualities, engendered mostly by the poor performance of Soviet troops in the 'Winter War' of 1939–40 against Finland, was profound, and OKH did not expect that either this period of warning or the known Soviet numerical superiority in tanks and aircraft would avail them anything. The Germans also knew that the Red Army had taken the retrograde step of disbanding its armoured divisions and redistributing their tanks in smaller formations among the infantry divisions – though in fact this measure was then being reversed in part, and new mechanised corps were being set up.

As it happened, events conspired to

give the Russians an even longer period of warning, but to throw away the advantage thus conferred, by ignoring the indications of an imminent German aggression until almost the last moment. At the end of March 1941 the pro-Axis government of Yugoslavia concluded an agreement with Nazi Germany. The agreement was rejected by the people in a spontaneous and violent uprising, which resulted in repudiation of the newly-signed treaty. Hitler flew into a violent rage at the insult to Germany, and ordered an immediate invasion of Yugoslavia and of Greece (where the Italian invasion had been repulsed). Forces for the invasion of the Balkans could only be found from those allocated to the 'Barbarossa' operation, which consequently had to be postponed. Yugoslavia was invaded on 6th April, and on the 7th OKH amended the Barbarossa timetable, stipulating that invasion of the Soviet Union would begin four to six weeks after the conclusion of the operations in southeast Europe. But by the time this amendment was issued most of the troops intended for Barbarossa (almost three echelons out of four envisaged) had already moved into Poland and East Prussia, and news of their presence had reached London via the agents of the Polish Home Army (the partisan movement owing allegiance to the Polish Government in exile). Winston Churchill notified Stalin of the accumulation of German strength along the Soviet borders in April. But Churchill had been an implacable opponent of Communism ever since 1917, had been a prime mover behind the intervention of British troops in the Russian Civil War of 1918–1922, and had favoured British and French participation on the side of Finland in its war with Russia of 1939–40. To Stalin, himself a devious and unscrupulous manipulator, information

Panzer general *par excellence:* Heinz Guderian in happy mood during the intoxicating months of victory

from such a source was bound to be tainted. He believed that Churchill's sole concern was to relieve the pressure on Great Britain by embroiling the Soviet Union in the war against Germany, and therefore ignored the warning. Given his nature, and Churchill's anti-Communist past, this behaviour was perhaps understandable even if inexcusable. What is less easy to comprehend is his refusal to credit similar reports coming from his own intelligence services, which he presumably regarded as more reliable than the British. His failure to act on these reports has never been satisfactorily explained by the Soviet historians, and any attempt to elucidate it must be largely speculative. It is, however, likely that realisation that the army was in a grossly unfit state to fight a war in the immediate future, and that he himself was primarily responsible for this state of affairs, influenced Stalin's attitude to reports which suggested the time of trial was already at hand.

By 1937 Stalin had succeeded in disposing of all the most likely rivals to himself for the political leadership of the country. The spirit of the Communist Party had been broken by years of purges, and it had become a cowed and submissive tool of his will. There remained, however, an alternative source of power, in the shape of the armed forces, and in 1937–38 Stalin had subjected the officer corps to a series of purges designed to reduce it to the same state of subservience as the Party apparatus. Before the purges began there were 300 officers of the rank of divisional commander or above; of these 183 were removed, all arrested and many shot, the rest being sent to prisons or concentration camps where they were subjected to forced labour and atrocious conditions, and where many of them died prematurely. The figure of 183 included three of the five Marshals of the Soviet Union, and thirteen of the fifteen Army Commanders (four star generals). No figures are available for the numbers of officers below general's rank who disappeared in the purges, but they certainly amounted to several thousand. Among those who were shot were the Chief of Staff, Marshal Tukhachevsky, a soldier of great ability who had pioneered the application of the German theories of armoured warfare in the Red Army, Marshal Blyukher, who had defeated the Japanese incursion into Soviet Far Eastern territory at Lake Hasan in 1938, and a number of the most talented thinkers and innovators in the Red Army. Their places were taken mostly by men who were more remarkable for their devotion to Stalin's person than for their military qualities – Voroshilov, Kulik, Mekhlis, and others – and the results of such leadership were soon to be seen in the lamentable performance put up by the Red Army against the grossly outnumbered Finns in the winter of 1939. Only by replacing Voroshilov as People's Commissar for Defence by Marshal Semyon Timoshenko (one of the few professional soldiers of high rank who retained his confidence) was Stalin able to bring the Finnish war to a successful conclusion – but not before the watching world had concluded, almost unanimously, that the Red Army was a 'paper tiger' incapable of standing up to a major antagonist.

There was, however, one outstanding exception to this pessimistic consensus – Japan, and since both the troops and the military leader who gave them cause to hold a different opinion were to play crucial roles in the Battle of Moscow, it is worth considering why Japan's view was at variance with world opinion. In 1938, at Lake Hasan on the border between Manchuria and the Soviet Far Eastern Maritime Province, Japanese forces encroached into Soviet territory. They were dislodged after some days of heavy fighting by the Siberian troops of the Far Eastern Red Banner Army – the army which in 1941 was to be transferred almost bodily to the west as the last large cadre formation available to defend Moscow. Japan made no further incursions into the Maritime Province, but in the following year a force about 75,000 strong occupied a salient of Mongolian territory along the Khalkhin Gol River. The People's Republic of Outer Mongolia invoked its defence agreement with the Soviet Union, and Soviet troops already stationed in Mongolia under the agreement were sent to the area. Reinforcements were also despatched from Russia, and a talented general, with a predominantly cavalry background, was assigned to command the force. Between 20th and 31st August 1939 he completely routed the Japanese, killing, wounding or capturing 41,000 of them, at a cost of some 10,000 casualties to his own troops. The general's name was Georgy Konstantinovich Zhukov; the Khalkhin Gol campaign was his first major combat triumph. His second, two-and-a-half years later, would be the Battle of Moscow. In it the Siberian troops would play an outstanding role, and their presence would be possible because Japan decided in 1941 to strike south against the colonial dependencies of the embattled European powers rather than north against the hard-pressed Soviet Union. An important factor in the Japanese decision would be the rough handling which its army had received in 1938 and 1939, especially the rout at Khalkhin Gol. Thus by defeating the Japanese in Mongolia in 1939, Zhukov affected the entire course of the Second World War, and in particular helped himself to win the Battle of Moscow.

However, the Khalkhin Gol campaign attracted little notice in Europe at the time (the Second World War broke out the day after the campaign ended), and any effect it might have had on military opinion was soon to be completely overshadowed by the near-fiasco of the Soviet invasion of Finland. Timoshenko was appointed to remedy the deficiencies of the army so blatantly exposed by that disastrous campaign, and he set about his task with forcefulness and skill. Talented officers who had been jailed in the purges were rehabilitated and promoted; they included a General Rokossovsky who was to become in due course a Marshal and one of the most successful Soviet field commanders. Zhukov himself, an old friend and colleague of Timoshenko's from their cavalry days, was given command of the important Kiev Special Military District, bordering on German-occupied Poland and in January 1941 was elevated to become Timoshenko's principal assistant in modernising the armed forces as Chief of the General Staff. The decision to disband the armoured divisions, shown by the German campaigns in Poland and France to be completely misconceived, was reversed, and a start was made with establishment of mechanised corps, combining tanks and motorised infantry as did the German system. But the task was so large – not the least difficult aspect of it was the restoration to the cowed officer corps of the morale without which initiative is hard to inculcate – that it could not conceivably be completed before 1942 at the very earliest. Stalin knew this, and it is most likely that when in early 1941 evidence began to come in showing that the Red Army would have to fight before it was ready, he wilfully thrust such evidence aside. The poor state of the army was mainly the result of his own actions; its numbers could be quickly increased by partial and unpublicised mobilisations, and these took place in early 1941. But to improve quality and morale would take much longer. Nothing in Stalin's life suggests that his conscience was a delicate one, but in the period April–June 1941, even he must have found himself difficult to live with, and the torpor into which he fell for several weeks after the beginning of the German invasion suggests that this was in fact the case.

Stalin persuaded himself that the

inevitable could be avoided. He determined, by appeasing Hitler to the utmost, to give him no 'excuse' to attack – that Hitler needed no excuse for his own part, and would fabricate one for consumption by the German people, was an unpleasant fact which he would not face, despite the experience of Poland, Denmark, Norway, Belgium, the Netherlands and Luxemburg. Deliveries of raw materials, including oil and minerals which in a few weeks would be used to power German tanks and provide the metal for their ammunition, continued. No provocation of any kind was to be afforded to the German military forces massing on the borders. A German reconnaissance aircraft force-landed deep in Soviet territory, and its crew failed to destroy the photographs which had been taken. When these had been developed, Timoshenko asked for permission to fire on these intruders. Stalin refused; it would be provoca-

tive. So day after day the Luftwaffe's spy planes droned undisturbed across the Soviet Union, perfecting the German intelligence cover. No German general must be given the excuse to start a war with the Soviet Union on his own initiative.

Despite their forced unpreparedness, the Soviet forces were large and possessed formidable potentialities. The population of the Soviet Union, at about 170 million, was twice that of Germany, and though Soviet sources have never disclosed the precise number of divisions under arms by the summer of 1941, it is thought that they totalled over 230. Many of these, however, particularly those in the interior of the country, were only partially embodied, and would not be made up to full strength (14,300 men) until a full mobilisation was decreed. The troops who would have to bear the initial brunt of the German attack were the 132 divisions of the Baltic, Western, Kiev and Odessa Military

Against the Japanese: Zhukov's crushing victory at Khalkhin Gol in August 1939 greatly enhanced his pre-war reputation in Moscow

Districts, rather less than the 155 expected in the German assessments, but a force which if properly trained, equipped and led should be capable of holding the 134 German divisions which were to be launched against it. Against that, however, were the poor state of training and morale, especially of officers, the lack of experience of Blitzkrieg in which the German forces were rich, and the fact that the invasion when it came, would catch the Red Army in the throes of re-organisation, with many of the infantry divisions below strength, and the newly reorganised tank divisions of the mechanised corps at less than half their war establishment. The Germans, in the event, were able to improve on their assessment of available forces and put into the field

141 divisions of their own (89 infantry, 51 Panzer or motorised and 1 cavalry), together with 14 Roumanian divisions, a Hungarian army corps of slightly more than two divisions, and in the north, the Finnish Army and the German Army of Norway contributed about 20 more divisions between them. The total Axis force was equivalent to 181 divisions and 18 brigades, of which about 160 divisions attacked on the main front between the Baltic and the Black Sea. In the number of combat-ready formations available from the start of hostilities, the Red Army was therefore outnumbered in manpower. In armour, however, it possessed a large numerical advantage, with thirty-four armoured divisions against the German twenty, but the tanks with which these divisions were equipped were for the most part inferior to the German PzKw 3 and 4, although two extremely formidable models, the KV heavy and T-34 medium, were just beginning to take

their places in the Soviet line. Once they were available in quantity, and their crews had become familiar with them, they would prove an extremely unpleasant surprise to the Wehrmacht. The T-34 in particular was a very advanced machine for its day, and even now in the late 1960s the medium tanks not only of the Soviet Army but of every tank-manufacturing country incorporate features which it was first to display. But in June 1941 it was neither abundant nor familiar, and therefore could have little impact on the impending clash of arms. Most of the Soviet armoured divisions were equipped with inferior tanks such as the BT-7 and T-26, and of the total force (which is believed to have numbered about 20,000, though the Soviets have never released a figure for its size, probably because of the humiliation involved in admitting to having been trounced by a German force which totalled only about 3,700 tanks), only about 8,000 were in an operational state when Germany struck, and less than 1,500 of those were of the new types.

In the case of the air forces, circumstances were rather similar. The air support provided by the Luftwaffe was organised into three '*Luftflotten*' (Air Fleets), Nos 1, 2 and 4, operating with Army Groups North, Centre and South respectively, and totalled approximately 5,000 aircraft. The Red Air Forces possessed about 12,000 aircraft of all types, most of which were available for use on the Soviet-German front. But in general they were of inferior characteristics to those of the Germans, and the pilots lacked experience. To make matters worse, the aircraft were not dispersed on receipt of warning of imminent attack (as they easily could have been, since the Western USSR can almost be regarded as one vast grass airfield), but remained parked wingtip to wing-tip on airfields already targetted by the reconnaissance flights, and were destroyed by the hundred in the early hours of hos-

tilities. There is reason to believe that over 1,200 were destroyed on 22nd June alone, most of them on the ground.

The manner in which the ground forces of the westernmost military districts were deployed during the early months of 1941 could hardly have been more suitable for the German style of warfare if OKH had been allowed to arrange it. Under the regime of Voroshilov bombastic assertions of invincibility had gone far to replace intelligent planning as the basis of military doctrine. The troops were taught that in the event of invasion they would at once hurl the enemy back from sacred Soviet soil and crush him on his own territory. This, coupled with the concept of war, derived from First World War experience, that envisaged it as linear and mainly static, had caused the forces to be distributed evenly along the length of the frontier, and to be deployed close to it. In any war, the defender is faced with the problem that he must guard against a breakthrough, at any point, whereas the attacker can concentrate in superior numbers at the points chosen for a breakthrough, even if his overall strength is inferior, but the chosen deployment of the Red Army for the battle of the frontiers left little in reserve for liquidating breakthroughs and rendered the entire covering force liable to encirclement and piecemeal destruction. To make matters worse still, many of the forces were not in fact in position, but were scattered over the terrain in the course of summer manoeuvres. That a sizeable element should be kept back from the frontiers was not in itself a bad thing, in view of the way in which the Wehrmacht planned to fight the campaign, but the formations behind the main defensive line did not in fact constitute any kind of coherent force, operating under an integrated plan, and, when hostilities did break out, the bulk of them were at once marched towards the sound of the guns, there to be encircled with their fellows.

Not until the afternoon of Saturday, 21st June, did Stalin decide finally that the evidence of German designs upon the Soviet Union could no longer be ignored. A meeting of the Politburo was held to decide what should be done, and at it the latest and most precise evidence, including the statements of German deserters that the attack was scheduled for the coming night, was presented. But Stalin still refused to believe that Hitler was about to treat him and the German-Soviet alliance with the cynicism with which he himself had treated so many obligations in the past. A mere six days previously he had authorised an official statement by TASS, the Soviet news agency, which denounced suggestions that a Soviet-German war impended. At the Politburo meeting he harped on the possibility that a German general, or a group of generals, might be plotting to force the hand of a reluctant Führer by tricking the Soviet Union into attacking by means of a 'provocation'. Eventually, however, it was agreed to alert the forces, order them to occupy defensive positions, disperse the aircraft, institute civil defence precautions and a black-out in the cities. But all was to be done in absolute secrecy, so as to provide no excuse for a 'provocation', and even if troops successfully repelled attacks they were in no circumstances to pursue their opponents into German-controlled territory. So secret were the instructions that no one was to know of them until they were ready for transmission, and this extraordinary circumspection made it necessary for Timoshenko and Zhukov to write out the telegrams themselves in Timoshenko's office, transmitting none until all had been written. The consequence of all this was that only the navy (whose Commander-in-Chief, Admiral Kuznetsov, took urgent steps through his own channels of communication as soon as he was told of the danger) received warning in time to act on it – and even there, difficulties occurred when the German bombers appeared over the naval bases, since the commanders of air defences, in the absence of instructions, refused in some cases to open anti-aircraft fire or order fighters aloft to defend the fleet which was under air attack before their eyes. The transmission of the alert order to the army and air force did not begin until well after midnight, too late to be implemented in the forward areas, and in many cases too late to be passed on to the lower formations before the German artillery bombardment and air strikes told them that the war had begun.

So at 3.30 am on Sunday, 22nd June 1941 – the 129th anniversary of Napoleon's invasion of Russia – an army which was tried, tested and ready for war attacked one which was none of these things. Within a matter of weeks the Soviet military structure lay in ruins, the bulk of its regular forces dead or in prisoner-of-war camps, along with hundreds of thousands of hastily mobilised reservists, the Germans had captured the third and fourth largest Soviet cities, Kiev and Kharkov, and stood at the gates of the only two larger ones, Moscow and Leningrad. It seemed that the hurricane which had enveloped France in the previous year was about to do the same to Russia. That it faltered, recoiled, and failed in its task of destruction was due to many factors. But one of the most important of them was the military genius and iron nerve of the architect of victory at Moscow, Stalingrad, Kursk, and Berlin – the forty-five year old General Zhukov who that night sat in the office of the People's Commissar of Defence, hastily filling in telegram forms. Of all the battles which confirmed his place in history as the supreme master of the 20th Century war of nations in arms, none was more crucial to the future of his country than the Battle of Moscow. And none was fought with slimmer resources.

From the frontier to Smolensk

The Wehrmacht was unleashed against Russia under a barrage of lies, as it had been against Poland nearly two years before. Both in Orders of the Day to the troops, and in statements to the German people the Nazi government justified the invasion as the pre-emption of an imminent Soviet attack upon Germany. But there is no need to waste sympathy upon the Stalin regime, which fully matched that of Hitler in its cynicism, and which had, indeed, used the same device, allegation of impending aggression, to justify its own attack upon Finland. When Molotov, on receiving the German declaration of war, asked the German Ambassador 'Do you think we deserved this?', he spoke not with the voice of outraged rectitude but with that of the conspirator betrayed. To this day Soviet histories describe Germany's aggression as a 'breach of faith', but gloss over the fact that it describes the situation accurately as not merely a transgression of international good manners but as a breach of an actual and formal alliance – an alliance with Nazism of which most Russians are somewhat ashamed.

Since, however, it is still sometimes said that the Nazi attack forestalled a Soviet one, and some (notably General Schmidt, the Chief of Staff of the German Sixth Army, later captured at Stalingrad) still maintain that this was the case, it may be worth considering what the situation actually was on the morning of 22nd June. In the first place, it is true that Soviet forces were deployed in strength along and behind the frontiers, and that some – though not nearly enough of them – were in a state of combat alert. These factors could be interpreted as evidence that the Red Army was making its preliminary dispositions for an invasion of German-occupied Poland. Equally, however,

the forward deployment can also be seen as deriving from the conservative Stalin-Voroshilov military doctrine which underestimated the effects of armoured forces, expected to repel aggression by linear defence and postulated that the successful defensive battles would be followed by a mighty linear counteroffensive, in which the enemy would be 'beaten on his own territory'. As for the fact that some forces were ready for battle, there is ample evidence from Soviet sources that in most cases the 'combat alert' was introduced by local commanders, usually without the knowledge of their superiors, that they were motivated by a profound uneasiness at what they could hear (in some cases could see) happening across the border, and that the most they were able to do was to move troops away from their barracks, so that they would not be bombed in their beds. This evidence is confirmed by a number of statements by German generals on the events of the first days, and even more by arguments which went on long before 'Barbarossa' was launched. The most respected of the older generals, Field-Marshal Gerd von Rundstedt, who commanded Army Group South, was strongly opposed to the invasion. Hitler attempted to convince him that Russia was planning to invade in the summer of 1941, but Rundstedt remained unpersuaded, and after the war said that on crossing the frontier he found no signs of offensive preparations in the forward area. In any event, the chaos which supervened in all levels of the Red Army when the invasion took place could hardly have occurred in an army which was on the verge of mounting its own operations. For every formation that was alerted, there were dozens which were not; mechanised corps without tanks, lorried infantry without lorries, artillery without ammunition, officers without orders. Had the Red Army really been on the verge of an invasion, its commanders would stand

Bock, C-in-C Army Group Centre. His target: Moscow

Rundstedt, C-in-C Army Group South. His target: Kiev

convicted as the most inept aggressors in the history of war. That Stalin expected sooner or later to have to fight Germany is incontestable, and Soviet sources do not tell whether he would have initiated the clash himself or waited for Germany to do so. But it is equally clear that he knew his army was not ready to fight, and would not be so until well into 1942. For him, and equally for Timoshenko and Zhukov, the war came approximately twelve months too early.

In the first days, it began to look as if the OKH intention, to annihilate the Red Army west of the Dvina-Dnieper line was fully capable of realisation. The forward deployment of the Soviet forces was admirably suited to the German desire for major encirclements, and persistence in standing fast (motivated as much by fear of the consequences of unauthorised, even if prudent, withdrawal, as by a desire to die in the last ditch) made the German task even easier. Stalin had the Commander-in-Chief of the Western Axis, General Pavlov, and his Chief of Staff, arrested and shot, which may have stiffened the will of some other generals, but certainly did nothing to improve their readiness to use their initiative. The force on the frontiers melted away into a series of

small, ragged formations, some of which, if fortunate enough to be led by strong-willed officers, managed to make their way out to the east through the coarse-meshed net of the encircling Panzer forces. Others, less fortunate, began the long trek to German prison camps, from which few would emerge when the war was over. Everywhere a sense of disorganisation bordering on panic prevailed. General Popel, leading the remnants of his XV Mechanised Corps to the east through the German operational rear, speaks of officers stealing or buying civilian clothing in the villages through which they passed, so that they could make their way to their homes and have done with the war, and tells of discovering, many miles behind the German lines, a lone Red Army private guarding a field full of undamaged Soviet tanks, not one of which had a drop of fuel in it.

For the Germans, the first three weeks of the war were a repetition of the Polish and French campaigns. Casualties were almost negligible, the dead, at 8,886 for the first ten days of the campaign averaging about six men per division per day, and the wounded less than twenty. Such a rate of attrition could be maintained almost indefinitely, certainly for a

Blitzkrieg campaign scheduled to last only four months. And given the way in which the Red Army's infantry was falling before the scythe of the Panzer armies, the campaign might not last that long.

However much the emphasis of the German campaign might vary, and the arguments between Hitler and his generals on this question are to be found in the next chapter, there was never any doubt on the Soviet side that Moscow was to be defended at all costs. The progress of Army Groups North and South was viewed with disquiet, but Army Group Centre's thrust on both sides of the main Brest-Moscow highway (one of the few surfaced roads to be found in the Soviet Union at that time) was looked on with the utmost alarm, because of the threat which it posed to the capital. At an average rate of advance of nearly thirty kilometres (eighteen miles) a day, Field-Marshal von Bock's troops, spearheaded by Panzer Groups 2 and 3, had penetrated almost to Smolensk by 10th July. If they reached that city, they would be 680 kilometres from their starting point at Brest Litovsk, a mere 420 kilometres from Moscow, and at that rate of progress would be there in another two weeks. It was imperative that they be stopped, or at the very least, substantially slowed.

The covering forces in the central sector of the front, the Third, Fourth and Tenth Armies, had been cut to pieces in the Bialystok and Minsk pockets, but mobilisation was now in full swing, and the STAVKA reserves were being directed to the Smolensk axis as fast as the hard-pressed railway system could take them. By 10th July the forces of Western Front, defending a line along the western Dvina and Dnieper rivers from Idritsa in the north to Rechitsa in the south comprised five armies – Thirteenth, Nineteenth, Twentieth, Twenty-first and Twenty-second – with a sixth (Sixteenth) in reserve, and the remains of the Fourth Army with-

drawing into the sectors held by the Thirteenth and Twenty-first Armies. However, the speed of the advance of Fourth Panzer Army to the Dvina and Dnieper rivers took the Red Army by surprise, with its defensive deployment incomplete, and large formations of Nineteenth, Twentieth and Twenty-first Armies still far from their assigned sectors. On Western Front's 500-mile sector only twenty-four divisions were in place, with 145 tanks in combat-worthy condition. Army Group Centre's Panzer forces had been worn down, more by the distances they had covered on bad roads than by the Red Army, but had between five and seven times this number in going order at the start of the battle. German air support, *Luftflotte* 2 had about 1,000 combat-worthy aircraft available, whereas the Soviet defenders had slightly under 400 still capable of use, from airfields strewn with the wrecks of twice that number, lost through the failure to disperse them before 22nd June. In guns and mortars, too, the Germans had an advantage, with 6,600 to 3,800. It had been a tenet of pre-war Soviet military doctrine that a line could be defended against a three to one superiority, but the Germans had disproved that so many times since September 1939 that few if any Soviet commanders could believe it by mid-July. Nevertheless, a major battle had to be fought along the Dvina-Dnieper line if Moscow was not to be placed in danger.

One factor which worked in the Red Army's favour was the German tendency to underestimate available Soviet reserves and the speed at which they could be mobilised. OKH believed that Western Front had only eleven combat-worthy divisions left, and expected that once these were smashed the road to Moscow would lie open. Consequently it neither deployed nor supplied for an extended engagement, while in addition it began to contemplate other contingencies. On 13th July, the day that

Guderian's troops penetrated to within eleven miles of Smolensk, he recorded the following other projects as under study at OKH. 1. An operation which would take his Panzer Group away from the Central axis to assist Army Group South. 2. A staff study of the forces to be left in the east to control the Soviet Union after it had been defeated. 3. A study of the dispositions of the German Army in Europe once 'Barbarossa' was over and it had been reduced in size. 4. The strategy of the African campaign, coordinated with an attack on the Suez Canal through Turkey and Syria. 5. Preliminary studies for an attack on the Persian Gulf through the Caucasus.

As Guderian commented bitterly after the war 'Such trains of thought take a man far from reality'. They were only possible in an organisation which believed the current campaign to be as good as over. And it was far from that, as Guderian's divisions were already discovering, with heavy casualties reported by 10th and 18th Panzer and 29th Motorised Divisions, very stiff Russian resistance, and large reinforcements moving up from the east.

The Battle of Smolensk opened formally on 10th July, when Panzer Groups 2 and 3 were launched from Vitebsk towards Dukhovshchina and Orsha towards Yelnya, in an attempt to dissect and encircle the Soviet Sixteenth, Nineteenth and Twentieth Armies in the centre of Timoshenko's front. Simultaneously the left flank forces of Panzer Group 3 advanced from their bridgeheads over the western Dvina towards Velikiye Luki, and Guderian's right wing moved forward on Roslavl.

The attacking forces at once ran into heavy resistance, with heavy

The height of folly: Russian aircraft, massed wing-tip to wing-tip on their airfields, were wiped out in their hundreds in the first hours of 'Barbarossa'

concentrations of artillery. Here too, on Twentieth Army's sector they first encountered a new Soviet weapon which was subsequently to become famous – the Katyusha rocket mortar. Marshal Yeremenko described the results; 'the effect of dozens of simultaneous explosions exceeded all our expectations. The enemy troops flung themselves into panic flight. But our troops who were in the front line near the explosions also came running back, because to preserve security none of them had been warned of our intention to use the new weapons.' In any event, there were not enough Katyushas available as yet to produce a decisive result, but, like the T-34 tank and the IL-2 Shturmovik ground attack aircraft, their mere existence was a danger signal. Russian ingenuity was not to be despised.

Nevertheless, the Germans persisted with their attacks, and the Soviet defence had soon been pierced at a number of places. At the northern end of the Smolensk axis, Twenty-second

Army was soon in serious trouble because its left flank became bared through withdrawals by its northern neighbour (Twenty-seventh Army of Northwestern Front) on 11th July, while Hoth's breakthrough towards Vitebsk forced the Twentieth Army, its southerly neighbour, away to the southeast, thus baring its right flank, to leave it isolated in the Polotsk fortifications and a bridgehead west of the Dvina. The six divisions of Twenty-second Army had to defend a frontage of 175 miles. On 12th and 13th July it came under attack from elements of some sixteen divisions of Army Groups North and Centre. By the 16th its front had been broken, Velikiye Luki and Vitebsk were in danger, and with them the entire flank and rear of the Soviet positions. General Konev had already counterattacked and stopped one German penetration with two divisions of his own Nineteenth Army, and elements of the adjacent Twentieth Army on 10th July, but the situation along the southern edge of the Smolensk axis was deteriorating too fast for such stop-gap measures to affect the situation. Guderian's Panzer Group 2 captured bridgeheads over the Dnieper south of Orsha and north of Novy Bykhov on the 11th, and the following morning struck out from them towards Smolensk and Krichev, outflanking the Soviet Thirteenth Army from north and south. Four of its infantry divisions and the remains of one mechanised corps (Twentieth) were soon cut off from the rest of the army, and remained in an isolated hedgehog position at Mogilev, where they occupied two of Guderian's Panzer Corps for two weeks until finally reduced, thus weakening his offensive towards Roslavl. The rest of Thirteenth Army, however, was forced away to east and southeast, and with it went any hope of containing the Germans west of the Dnieper, unless they could be forced to turn back by a threat to their rear.

Timoshenko had already seen the possibility of using such a threat, and

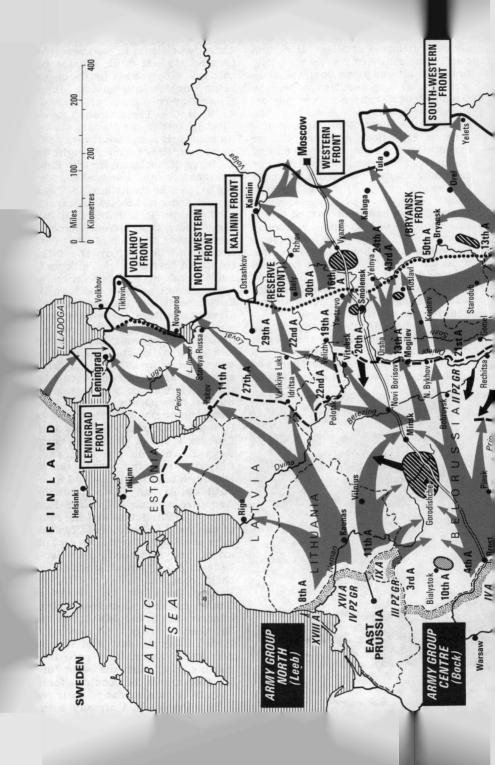

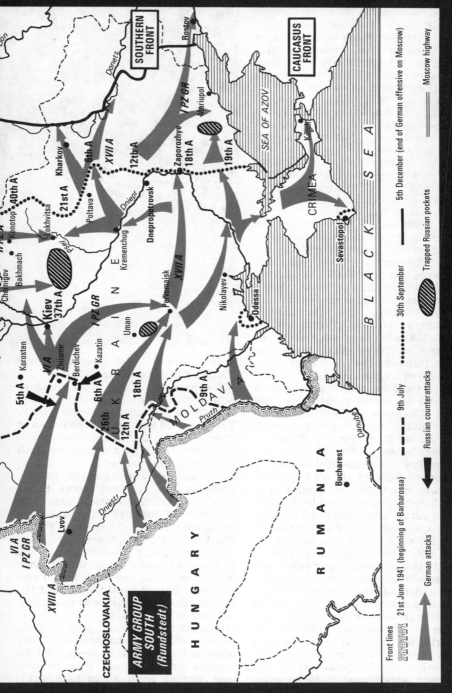

The Battlefronts: 2nd June–5th December 1941

CAUCASUS
FRONT

SOUTHERN
FRONT

ARMY GROUP
SOUTH
(Rundstedt)

Front lines

␣␣␣␣␣ 21st June 1941 (beginning of Barbarossa)

•••• 9th July

•••• 30th September

━━━━ 5th December (end of German offensive on Moscow)

▓ Trapped Russian pockets

◀ Russian counterattacks

◀ German attacks

──── Moscow highway

Don

Rostov

Donets

SEA OF AZOV

CRIMEA

Sevastopol

Kerch

B L A C K   S E A

Mariupol

Zaporozhye
18th A

19th A

12th A

XVII A

6th A

Kharkov

21st A

40th A

Konotop

Chernigov
Bakhmach

Lokhvitsa

Poltava

Dniepr

Dnepropetrovsk

Kremenchug

Pervomaisk

Nikolayev

Odessa

Danube

Bucharest

R U M A N I A

Pruth

M O L D A V I A
9th A

Dniestr

Lvov

CZECHOSLOVAKIA

H U N G A R Y

U K R A I N E

Uman

Kazatin

Berdichev

Zhitomir

Korosten

Kiev
37th A

Psel

II PZ A

XVII A

I PZ GR

VI A

5th A

6th A
18th A

26th
12th A

XVIII A

VI A
I PZ GR

III PZ GR

Caucasus Front

on 13th October he directed General Gerasimenko's Thirteenth Army to cross to the west bank of the Dnieper and attack northwestwards towards Bobruysk, athwart Guderian's lines of communication. This new attack caused considerable worry to the generals of Army Group Centre, especially to Guderian, whose forces were becoming extended further and further to the east. His 29th Motorised Division captured Smolensk on 16th July, but his right flank XXIV Panzer Corps was under heavy attacks from Thirteenth Army. However he decided not only to maintain his objectives, but withdrew XLVI Panzer Corps to assist Hoth and Panzer Group 3 in destroying the divisions of the Soviet Twenty-second Army encircled northeast of Smolensk. In the event, his confidence was justified, to the extent that Thirteenth Army's attack failed of its object, but the eastward drive to Roslavl, Yelnya and Dorogobuzh inevitably lost most of its impetus.

STAVKA in its turn was alarmed at the loss of Smolensk and the breaching of the Dnieper line, so Timoshenko was ordered to restore the situation. Further reserves were dispatched to him, and an entire second line, the 'Front of Reserve Armies', was set up behind that of Western Front, along a line running from Staraya Russa to Bryansk by way of Ostashkov and Yelnya. It was commanded at first by Lieutenant-General I A Bogdanov (who was nominated to command it on 14th July, but replaced by Zhukov on the 30th), and comprised no less than six new Armies – Twenty-fourth, Twenty-eighth, Twenty-ninth, Thirtieth, Thirty-first and Thirty-second – two of which (Thirty-first and Thirty-second) were maintained as a reserve behind the others. Though weak in aircraft (it had only 153 in combat-worth condition) it was nevertheless a noteworthy addition of strength to the crumbling Western Front. Soon however, further deterioration of the position on the Smolensk axis forced it to be com-

mited in part to an over-ambitious attack, which began on 25th July.

The purpose of this attack was to relieve the main forces of Western Front by attacking from Bely, Yartsevo and Roslavl, on the flanks of Panzer Group 2, towards Smolensk, recapture the city, and join up with Western Front west of it. Five army-sized groups were formed by re-grouping five of the Reserve Front armies, and they comprised four tank and sixteen infantry divisions. The remaining army of Reserve Front, Thirty-second, was transferred to a new army group (the Front of the Mozhaysk Defence Line), whose other forces comprised yet another two new armies, Thirty-third and Thirty-fourth. The new Front was to occupy the defensive positions known as the Mozhaysk Defence Line, prepare anti-tank obstacles both ahead of the positions and behind them, and to prepare an additional rear defence line running from Nudol to Vysoki-

nichi. That alarm over the danger to Moscow was becoming acute is attested by this step; Mozhaysk is less than sixty miles west of Moscow, and General Artemyev, who was appointed to head the new army group, was the Commander of the Moscow Military District.

From the German side, the Smolensk battle was not proceeding unsatisfactorily towards the end of July, though the Soviet stand was proving harder to break than had been expected, and it was clear that the expectation of an open road between Smolensk and Moscow had been over-optimistic. Elsewhere on the immense front, however, matters were not wholly encouraging. Army Group North had stalled temporarily on the Luga River, while Army Group South, although close to Kiev, also appeared for the moment to have lost its impetus. Hitler at this time appeared increasingly to favour diversion of effort from the Moscow axis to the

Dazed, barefoot, half-dressed: the first Russian prisoners

achievement of decisions on the flanks, but before any diversion could take place Bock (whose personal interest in keeping up the pressure along Army Group Centre's front was heightened by the feeling that Hitler would be more inclined to remove forces from him if they appeared to be doing nothing) intensified the pressure on the isolated Soviet Twenty-second Army. He forced it out of the Polotsk fortifications and it retired to the northeast. Behind it fast-moving Panzer forces captured the town and junction of Velikiye Luki on 20th July, thus threatening its withdrawal route, but a hastily-organised Soviet counterattack on the next day drove them out. With this respite Twenty-second Army succeeded in making an orderly withdrawal across the Lovat river. By 27th July it had dug itself in on the east bank, where it succeeded in maintaining its positions, despite German attempts to outflank it from the south, until the end of August, and by so doing it protected the adjacent Northwestern Front from flank penetration during some crucial weeks for the defenders of the Leningrad area.

For both the German and Soviet staffs, the Smolensk axis – the direct route to Moscow – remained the crucial one, and Bock decided to eliminate the Soviet Armies, Sixteenth and Twentieth, guarding the approach to Vyazma, the next large town after Smolensk on the direct road and rail lines to the capital. Unknown to him, the Soviets had decided on a course of action which was to dovetail neatly into his proposed attack. Bock was fortunate in this respect; the same thing was to happen to him when in the following year, as Commander-in-Chief of Army Group South he found that Timoshenko's forces were advancing into encirclement. STAVKA had decided as a matter of operational convenience that an additional Army Group headquarters should be formed to handle the fighting along the lower reaches of the Berezina river, leaving Western Front in charge of that in the Smolensk area and along the River Sozh. On 24th July, therefore, a new 'Central Front', under Colonel-General FI Kuznetsov, was set up, and the Thirteenth and Twenty-first Armies of Western Front were resubordinated to it. Thus Western Front could now concentrate on what STAVKA still saw as its necessary task, the recapture of Smolensk, and proceeded to undertake this as soon as relieved of responsibility for the Berezina sector. Thus on 23rd July, from Roslavl, and 24th–25th July from the Bely and Yartsevo areas, Timoshenko launched the Sixteenth and Twentieth Armies westwards, just as Bock released his Panzers eastwards into their rear. By 27th July Sixteenth

Russian refugees; abandoned Russian tank

Army had captured Smolensk railway station, and was fighting in the northern suburbs of the city, while Twentieth Army was close to its eastern limits, but by then both armies were encircled. Timoshenko ordered them to reverse fronts and fight their way out to the east, but large numbers of them failed to do so, and though neither army was eliminated completely, they returned to the Soviet lines during 4th and 5th August with a very much reduced capability for further fighting. By then there had been a development which would have relieved the harassed Soviet commanders, had they known of it. On 30th July, Hitler had issued Directive 34, ordering Army Group Centre to abandon the advance on Moscow and go on to the defensive. The first phase of the Smolensk battle had ended. Soviet losses had been immense, (over 300,000 were captured, 3,200 tanks destroyed) but the Führer's doubts over the relative importance of the three major strategic targets had been given a new lease of life by the difficulties of advancing in the centre. Instead Panzer Group 3 was to assist in achieving a decision in the Leningrad area, and Panzer Group 2 to go to the aid of Army Group South.

None of this was known to STAVKA, and as it had never doubted that Moscow must be the main German objective it assumed that the unsuccessful frontal assault was to give place to an outflanking manoeuvre against the capital from north and south. The decision was therefore taken to put three of Western Front's armies into an attack against the German Ninth Army which formed the northern wing of Army Group Centre, and was therefore considered to be in possession of the jumping-off area for the northern claw of any such pincer movement. To disrupt the southern claw in a similar way the 'Front of Reserve Armies' was renamed 'Reserve Front' and placed under command of Zhukov on 30th July with orders to wipe out the

Above: Germans waiting, prior to another attack. *Right:* Prisoners, prisoners, prisoners

Germans in the Yelnya salient, which jutted out into the flanks of Western Front. To guard against a possibility that the southern claw of any attempted pincer movement on Moscow would come further south, through Bryansk and along the main road and railway from Kiev, another new army group, Bryansk Front, was set up, under the command of Lieutenant-General AI Yeremenko, with the Thirteenth and Fiftieth Armies. This front came into being on 14th August.

Although the issuing of Directive 34 brought an end to the direct assault on Moscow for the time being, it did not signify a general subsidence of the fighting on the central axis from the German side. Assistance to Army Group South involved *inter alia* the defeat of Central Front, which covered

the northern flank of the Soviet forces in the Ukraine, and the projecting right wing of Central Front (Twenty-second Army's front along the Lovat river) was to be driven back from its outflanking position north of Army Group Centre.

The German and Soviet offensives began almost simultaneously in the first days of August, with Sixteenth, Twenty-fourth and Thirtieth Armies of Western Front attacking the German Ninth Army with very limited success throughout the month. Ninth Army withdrew to the western bank of the Vop river, and there held on without great difficulty. Soviet official historians justify these operations by claiming that they tied Ninth Army down and prevented its being used elsewhere, but OKH was not in fact planning to use it anywhere else, and was not in any dire need of its services; their shortcomings derived from the

fact that only twenty per cent of their forces were of high mobility, and Ninth Army belonged to the other eighty per cent, the ordinary infantry, with much of its transport horse-drawn, which was not in short supply that summer. The conclusion cannot be avoided that the Soviet offensive was of very little utility, and this conclusion is reinforced by the revised assignments given to Western, Reserve and Bryansk Fronts on 25th August.

On the 22nd the Germans attacked strongly at the junction between Twenty-second and Twenty-ninth Armies, with the object of encircling the Soviet forces in the Velikiye Luki area and along the Lovat river. By the following day most of Twenty-second Army had been surrounded, and it escaped eastwards only at the cost of heavy casualties and the loss of most of its heavy equipment. Twenty-ninth Army folded back on its neighbours, and the Germans were eventually halted along the upper course of the western Dvina river.

The new assignments issued by STAVKA on 25th August to Western, Bryansk and Reserve Fronts still aimed at the recapture of Smolensk, but by drawing Reserve Front into the Smolensk operations implicitly acknowledged the inadequacies of the earlier attacks by the three Western Front armies. Western Front was to continue attacking northeast of Smolensk and to cooperate with Reserve Front in attaining the line Velizh-Demidov-Smolensk by 8th September. Reserve Front was to use the two armies of its left wing to expel the Germans from the Yelnya salient, while its remaining armies continued to work on the fortification of the Ostashkov-Kirov line of defences. Bryansk Front was to attack on 2nd September and advance south of Krichev, thus threatening the Germans at Smolensk with an outflanking movement from the south.

Of all these operations, the only one that could be claimed as successful was Zhukov's attack on the Yelnya salient, for though the Soviet losses were very large, and the German forces escaped encirclement by a narrow margin, the operational objective, elimination of the salient, was attained and German losses, too, were heavy. So hard pressed for reserves

Distraught women watch their beaten fathers, husbands and sons trudging west, bound for years of misery in German prison camps

Hande hoch! —two bewildered
Russian soldiers surrender a Stalin
Line strongpoint to their German
captors

was Guderian that at one point he was
forced to commit his headquarter
guard, and on 13th August he proposed
that the salient 'which now had no
purpose (because of the temporary
abandonment of the advance on
Moscow) and was a continual source
of casualties, be abandoned'. His
proposal was rejected by both Bock
and OKH, but on 5th September
Fourth Army was ordered to abandon
the salient nevertheless. With its
abandonment the shortened German
line became easier to defend. Zhukov
persisted with attacks on it for
several more days, but on 12th September Stalin despatched him to take
charge at Leningrad, where a total
collapse appeared to be imminent.
Western Front had been ordered on to
the defensive on 10th September, and
Reserve Front received similar orders
on the 16th. Catastrophe was impending in the south, too, and it was
necessary to husband the strength in
the centre.

So ended the Battle of Smolensk.
Soviet losses had been large, but the
outcome had not been entirely unsatisfactory. It could not be claimed
that the Germans had been stopped,
but their daily rate of advance had
been slowed from the eighteen to
twenty miles of the first three weeks
to four or five miles or less in August,
and in places, as at Velikiye Luki and
Yelnya, they had been forced to
retreat. As their rate of advance had
gone down, so had their casualties
increased, not spectacularly, but to
nine dead and thirty-two wounded per
division per day. In short, for a
seventy-five per cent reduction in rate
of advance, the German Army was
paying with fifty per cent increased
casualties. And its main aim–destruction of the Red Army west of the
Dnieper-Dvina line–had been shown to
be unattainable.

Cannae on
the Dnieper

It has already been said that many of the senior generals of the German Army – including the Commander-in-Chief Field-Marshal von Brauchitsch, the Chief of General Staff of the Army Colonel-General Halder, and Rundstedt himself – had opposed the invasion of Russia, and that Hitler had therefore planned to bring about a quick decision by destroying the bulk of the Red Army before it could retreat across the Dnieper.

This decision brought large problems in its train. It demanded quick encirclement of large forces, with the danger that large holes were left in the ring, through which much of the Red Army could punch its way out. To achieve encirclements of the requisite size, without leaving such holes, the Panzer forces of two army groups must be used. Otherwise Germany would have to settle for more modest encirclements; but this meant leaving large parts of the Red Army free from encirclement. However, only Army Group Centre had two Panzer Groups, hence no large encirclement could be mounted without its participation, except where the enemy could be pinned against the coast at the extremities of the Front. Encirclements in the centre, on the other hand, could be carried out by Army Group Centre without calling on either of the other army groups for assistance. Thus Army Group Centre was the key to any discussion of strategic objectives.

There were three particularly enticing prizes, one for each of the army groups. For Army Group North there was Leningrad, birthplace of the October Revolution which had brought the Communists to power in 1917, former capital of the Russian Empire, second city of the Soviet Union, major industrial centre and the main

Colonel-General von Kleist: his Panzer Group I was now to become the southern claw of the greatest manoeuvre of encirclement in the Wehrmacht's history

base of the Baltic Fleet. For Army Group Centre there was Moscow, the capital, also a major industrial centre, main focal point of European Russia's rail and road links, and a Holy City not merely of Communism but of 'Mother Russia' too. Army Group South's major target was Kiev, the third largest city in the Soviet Union, a large industrial centre in itself, but also the key to the even larger Kharkov industrial region, a major source of Soviet heavy industry, coal and oil. Because of the sparseness of the Soviet rail and road systems, most of the oil and petrol from the Caucasus also had to pass through the eastern end of this region on its way to the rest of the Soviet Union. The three cities were thus all prime political and economic objectives, whose importance to the Soviet Union was such that none could be left undefended. To attack them would ensure that the main forces of the Red Army were committed to battle and Stalin and STAVKA were helping to place the noose round the Red Army's neck by their insistence on linear defence and futile frontal attacks. With their opposition to strategic withdrawal, they were playing right into Hitler's hands by holding the Red Army forward.

Hitler was already beginning to accord higher priority to the Ukraine than to Moscow and Leningrad, when he said on 8th July that in any case he intended to raze both Moscow and Leningrad to the ground – something which he considered could be done by aircraft alone – and that for the moment Panzer Group 2, on the southern wing of Army Group Centre, should continue eastwards, so that the Moscow direction would be covered if it was later necessary for part of Army Group Centre to turn south. Thus he shelved a decision for the moment.

On the same day Halder presented to him a highly optimistic Intelligence assessment, claiming that 89 of the 164 known Soviet divisions had already been destroyed, and that of the remainder, 18 were on secondary fronts, 11 unknown, and only 46 known to be still combat-worthy. Brauchitsch then made a modest proposal that the success at Berdichev be exploited by turning Kleist's Panzers south into the rear of the Soviet Sixth and Twelfth Armies, to achieve a 'small decision'.

Hitler, on the other hand, favoured the seizure of Kiev and an advance down the west bank of the Dnieper, so as to achieve a 'big decision'. Brauchitsch objected that this was impossible because of supply difficulties, and Hitler conceded that first of all the strength of the opposition at Kiev would have to be ascertained. And there, for the moment, the matter was allowed to rest in the capable hands of Rundstedt. He dispatched Kleist to Kazatin, which was captured on 15th July. Southwest Front's only close-up lateral railroad was cut by this manoeuvre, and Budenny began to withdraw into the Dnieper bend.

But the troublesome Soviet Fifth Army remained at Korosten, and its presence continued to dim the glittering picture conjured up by Kiev, Ukrainian coal, industry and agriculture. Something would have to be done about it, and the matter was raised with Hitler on 17th July.

The outcome was OKW Directive 33 of 19th July. This ordered that after completing the operations at Smolensk, Panzer Group 2 and the infantry of German Second Army should turn southeast to destroy the Soviet Twenty-first Army (which was opposite the right wing of Army Group Centre), and then in co-operation with Army Group South should destroy the Soviet Fifth Army. At the same time, a concentric attack by Army Group South was to drive across the rear of the Soviet Sixth and Twelfth Armies and destroy them as well. The remaining Panzer forces of Army Group Centre, Group 3, were to move northeastwards to assist Army Group North, leaving the advance on Moscow to be continued by the infantry armies of Army Group Centre only.

This decision was tantamount to abandoning decisive operations against the main Soviet forces in the centre. The collapse of their neighbours on the northwest and southwest Fronts would force the Soviets to continue retreating, but there would be no more major encirclements of them by the Germans in the centre.

Two days later Hitler, paying his first visit to his armies in the east, appeared at HQ Army Group North, where he exposed some of his reasoning. It was essential to take Leningrad soon, in order to stop interference by the Soviet Baltic Fleet with the iron ore shipments from Sweden to Germany. Panzer Group 3 would therefore assist Army Group North by cutting the Leningrad-Moscow railway in order to hinder the transfer of Soviet forces to or from the area; this task must be undertaken as soon as Panzer Group 3 was available – that is, in about five days time. As for Moscow he didn't care, as 'Moscow for me is only a geographical concept'. Because of the general situation and the 'instability of the Slav character' the fall of Leningrad could bring about a complete collapse of Soviet resistance.

On 23rd July another conference took place between Hitler, Brauchitsch, and Halder, at which Halder reported that the Red Army forces now facing Germany numbered ninety-three Divisions of which thirteen were armoured. None of the participants seems to have commented on the fact that in the fifteen days since his previous report – fifteen days of hard and successful operations by the Wehrmacht – the Soviet forces had apparently almost doubled. But clearly, as Halder's own diary shows, the fierceness of the Russian resistance was beginning to make an impression. Despite Hitler's talk two days earlier of the possibility of an imminent Russian collapse, a note of uncer-

tainty began to creep into the conversation. Halder reported that the combat capability of the German infantry divisions was eighty per cent of what it had been on 22nd June, but that the Panzers were down to fifty per cent, that Army Group South would be over the Dnieper by mid-August, that very strong resistance was to be expected in the Moscow direction – and that the operations of Army Group North seemed to be a failure.

Hitler then emphasised that he believed in destroying the enemy wherever he could be found, but expressed the view that the Panzer formations could come in only at a later stage when there was no longer any great danger to rearward communications. Brauchitsch's disquiet over the more ambitious encirclements had begun to communicate itself to the Führer; after one month's fighting it was becoming clear that the Russian campaign would perhaps

Hitler decides: the Ukraine must be conquered before Moscow. Rundstedt (right) looks sceptical

be different from the 'manoeuvres with live ammunition' of 1939 and 1940

Hitler had that day issued a supplement to Directive 33, laying down future tasks. For Army Group South he ordered the crossing of the Don in the direction of the Caucasus after seizure of the Kharkov industrial region – a task which Army Group South still had to carry out. Brauchitsch protested that the new supplement was quite impossible in view of the current situation at the front, and asked that it be withdrawn until present operations had been concluded; when OKW refused, he raised the question with the Führer.

While Hitler refused to wait until the next battle had been won before contemplating the next but one, he took the opportunity to expound his views on the way mobile battles should be fought, now that there was some experience of fighting the Red Army; while the enemy resists stubbornly, is being decisively led, and has forces available for counterstrokes, no operations with far-reaching aims should be carried out. The Panzer forces should confine themselves to small encirclements, thus giving the infantry a chance to consolidate success quickly, and freeing the Panzer forces for new missions.

In brief, while the aims were to remain grandiose, the means of attaining them were to be scaled down. But while he was no doubt wise to take account of Halder's report that the Panzer forces had been reduced in one month to fifty per cent of the strength with which they had started, it does seem that a commensurate scaling-down of aims was needed if Hitler was to avoid the charge of instability of character which he had himself so recently levelled at the Slavs.

Brauchitsch and Halder went away disgruntled, and wrote a minute, in which they set out their views. To attack Moscow with infantry alone would be difficult but possible, provided quick results were not looked for, but a decisive offensive against the capital would require Panzer Groups 2 and 3, neither of which would now be available until early September. Thus Hitler's plan would present the enemy with a month's grace in which to collect new forces and build and occupy new defence lines. Moreover, the large Soviet group of forces in front of Moscow constituted a threat to the flanks of the other army groups and forced a dispersion of forces to guard against it as long as it remained in being. As to the idea of destroying Moscow from the air, there was no immediate expectation that the Luftwaffe would acquire bases near enough to operate on the necessary scale.

OKH asked once again for a re-

Left: German sappers fell trees
Above: German soldier and prisoner

examination of the tasks set to Army Group Centre, while admitting that there might be decisive economic factors unknown to them (Hitler was given to saying that his generals knew nothing about economics, and to exploiting their ignorance by citing economic factors to justify military decisions with which they disagreed). Naturally, OKH would do what it was told, but it had great misgivings about the possible consequences. Clearly, the Soviet objective was to last out until the winter, and if they succeeded, then next spring Germany would have to face more new armies and could be involved in the war on two fronts which it had hoped to avoid. Surely, OKH argued, the best way out would be to attack Moscow. The Soviets would have to stand and fight there, so there would be no question of their armies escaping yet again. And if Germany won the battle she would possess the seat of government, the important industrial centre, and the heart of the rail system. Russia would be cut in two. An aim as important as this must take precedence over smaller operations designed to cut up part of the Red Army.

The minute was firm and cogent, though deferential, and argued its case well. General Jodl even tried to strengthen its arguments by remarking that since the Soviets would inevitably stand and defend it, an attack on Moscow would be merely an expression of the Führer's own dictum that the enemy's 'living force' must be attacked wherever it could be found.

But the minute was never sent. Even as the German High Command was debating whether it could kill the Soviet bear in the next two months, or would have to be content with crippling it, Marshal Timoshenko hurled several newly raised armies into a counteroffensive in the centre,

57

attempting to relieve the large pocket of forces surrounded at Smolensk. All thoughts of Moscow, Kiev, and Leningrad had to be put aside for the time being, and swift improvisation became the order of the day.

The Russian attacks failed in their immediate objective – to wrest the initiative from Army Group Centre and relieve the trapped Soviet Sixteenth and Twentieth Armies. The Russians were ill-prepared, and there were still too many futile frontal attacks, with new forces committed piecemeal – probably because Timoshenko was not aware of the degree to which the Germans were stretched, and thus was led to over-estimate the immediate danger to Moscow. But the mere readiness to attack, and the appearance of large numbers of new formations, intensified still more the divisions of opinion among the German High Command, and led to further diversion of effort.

The first fruit of the hasty Soviet

Above: **German platoon moves up**
Right: **Machine-gun crew on the watch**

counteroffensive was a meeting of army commanders of the German Army Group Centre on 27th July at Novy Borisov. Guderian arrived, expecting to be ordered to push on to Moscow – or at least to Bryansk – but found instead a memorandum from Brauchitsch explicitly ruling out either possibility and stating that the first priority was destruction of the Soviet forces 'in the Gomel area' – that is, the Soviet Fifth Army.

Guderian was astounded. That he, the man whose studies and labour had given Germany the forces with which he himself had then conquered most of Europe, should be asked to turn in his tracks and 'advance' back towards Germany, to finish off forces which should have been dealt with by the infantry, was unthinkable. Brauchitsch was, of course, merely implementing Hitler's cautions about ambitious encirclements mentioned in discussion of Directive 33, but Guderian knew nothing of this except for what he gleaned in a disjointed fashion from the officers at the Army Group HQ. Of these, the man whom he knew to be least enthusiastic about his armoured dashes was Field-Marshal von Kluge, Commander-in-Chief of Fourth Army, to whom Guderian was uneasily and reluctantly subordinate. It is unlikely, therefore, that Guderian realised the full extent of the debate, or all the factors involved in it, and he left the conference in a mood of wounded pride, only partially assuaged by the fact that Panzer Group 2 was renamed 'Army Group Guderian', and made subordinate, not to Kluge, but to the Commander-in-Chief of Army Group Centre.

This new freedom from the restraints imposed by Kluge – a man of some guile, known in the Army as 'Kluger Hans' ('Crafty Hans') and not one to inspire loyalty in his colleagues – was used by Guderian to distort and wilfully misinterpret the directions he had been given at Novy Borisov. He was convinced that the main threat to Army Group Centre was not the Soviet Fifth Army in his deep rear, but the forces assembling on his right flank north of Roslavl, and he continued to believe this 'irrespective of any decisions Hitler might now take'.

This threat which he perceived took the form of a grouping described by STAVKA as the 'Group of Forces of Twenty-eighth Army', under the command of Lieutenant-General Kachalov, which had been assembled to help relieve the Smolensk pocket. Guderian proposed to Bock that Roslavl be captured, on the grounds that its seizure would give mastery of routes to the east, south, and south-west, thus making available a number of possibilities for continuing the offensive, and was allotted additional forces (the four divisions of VII Army

Corps). To relieve Panzer divisions withdrawn from the Yelnya bulge for use in the Roslavl operation, XX Army Corps (two divisions) was earmarked. Guderian was also given a cavalry division.

The necessary preparations took some days, and during this period Guderian received several visitors. On 29th July Hitler's chief adjutant, Colonel Schmundt, arrived, ostensibly to present Guderian with the Oak Leaves to his Iron Cross, but really to discuss his plans with him. He indicated that Hitler had not yet decided between Leningrad, Moscow, and the Ukraine. There is no evidence to show whether Schmundt was being particularly discreet or particularly stupid, since Hitler had in fact been indicating his lack of interest in Moscow for some time and was the very next day to issue Directive 34, which ordered Army Group Centre to cease its advance on the Soviet capital and go on to the defensive.

Guderian took advantage of the opportunity to urge a direct push on Moscow and also to put in a bid for new tanks and tank engines. On the 31st, the OKH liaison officer, Major von Bredow, turned up to report that 'OKH and the Chief of General Staff are engaged in a thankless undertaking, since the conduct of all operations is being controlled from the very highest level. Final decisions on the future course of events have not yet been taken'. Put more simply, this was a complaint about Hitler's interference, and a tacit invitation by OKH to Guderian to influence decisions not yet taken by his own actions.

The attack on Roslavl was launched on 1st August. By 3rd August, the town was in German hands, with 38,000 prisoners and 200 guns, and by 8th August all resistance had ceased. It had been a brilliant and rapid victory, but its very ease, and the small number of guns taken, should have shown Guderian that he had been wrong. This was no force assembled to pose a major threat. Rather it was a

hastily assembled scratch team, not much more than three divisions plus support elements – small indeed, by the standards of the Eastern Front – but neither Guderian nor any other German general has to date even remarked on this aspect of the Roslavl diversion.

Eleven days had now elapsed since the decision had been taken to eliminate the Soviet Fifth Army, and nothing had been done about it. Not even the closing of the Smolensk battle on 5th August – with the Soviet Sixteenth Army and XXIII Mechanised Corps wiped out, along with parts of the Nineteenth and Twentieth Armies, 300,000 prisoners, 3,200 tanks and 3,100 guns taken – could compensate for this failure.

Nor had the Roslavl episode contributed to easing the task of Army Group South. All it had done was to keep the Moscow option open, by maintaining Panzer Group 2 forward. Its effects on the battle for 'right-bank Ukraine' now remain to be considered.

Hitler had ordered the closing of the Uman pocket on 24th July. Although Kleist had wanted something more ambitious – namely to encircle Kiev from the south with one corps, and send his other two corps plunging down across the rear of both Southwest and South Soviet Fronts – he complied with the directive, apparently without protest. On 30th July, Panzer Group 1 struck deep into the columns of Red Army troops withdrawing from the pocket, wheeled towards the southwest, and on 3rd August linked up with the forward elements of Colonel-General von Stülpnagel's Seventeenth Army near Pervomaisk, enclosing two Soviet armies (Sixth and Twelfth), and parts of another (Eighteenth) – a total of fifteen infantry and five armoured divisions. Though some of the Soviet formations succeeded in fighting their way out, resistance in the pocket ended on 8th August. About 100,000 prisoners were taken, together with the commanders of the two trapped armies (Generals Muzychenko

The 122mm howitzer M1938 remained in Soviet first-line service throughout the war and for some years afterwards; it is a workmanlike and conventional weapon and, like most Soviet guns, exhibits considerable range for its weight. *Weight:* 2.2 tons. *Range:* 12,900 yards. *Shell weight:* 48lbs HE. *Rate of fire:* about eight to ten rounds per minute

Soviet 107mm Mortar M1938, used for heavy support of infantry; it was standard for many years. A shock absorber was incorporated in the mounting in order to reduce the tendency of the base plate to bury itself in soft ground. *Weight in action:* 344lbs. *Range:* 6,900 yards. *Bomb weight:* 19.8lbs. *Rate of fire:* twenty to twenty-five rounds per minute

The Soviet 82mm Mortar M1937 – a standard and ubiquitous weapon of Soviet Infantry which remained in service many years – is a conventional smooth-bore, drop-fired mortar, firing a finned bomb. *Weight in action:* 126lbs. *Range :* 3,280 yards with light bomb, 1,350 yards with heavy bomb. *Bombs:* HE 7.52 lbs or 15.4lbs. *Rate of fire:* twenty to thirty rounds per minute

and Ponedelin), 317 tanks, and 1,100 guns.

At the southern end of the front, where the main weight was to be carried by the Roumanian Third and Fourth Armies, events at first moved slowly, but the withdrawal of Soviet forces into the Uman pocket left South Front very thin on the ground, and by 5th August, Odessa was under siege, and accessible only by sea. The situation in the south was perilous for the Red Army, and Soviet reserves began to pour into the area. But STAVKA was already learning from its earlier mistakes. This time there was to be no piecemeal commitment of half-trained divisions. The new divisions (ten to Southwest Front, twelve to South Front, and two into Front Reserve) were mostly put into preparing a defensive line along the east bank of the Dnieper, and to helping remove industrial equipment, to set it up in the east, or at any rate to ensure that it did no work for Germany.

As to the Red Army itself, there must be no more mass surrenders of encircled formations, and steps were taken to ensure that the troops were indoctrinated to this effect.

Hitler, meanwhile, was again having difficulties with his generals, particularly those of Army Group Centre, on whom Moscow continued to exert a fatal attraction. On 4th August he arrived at Novy Borisov to hold a rather unusual 'conference': rather than allow professional solidarity to work upon him, he interviewed the army commanders separately, beginning with Halder's representative, Colonel Heusinger, and following with Bock, Guderian, and Hoth.

Though all recommended an advance on Moscow, Bock claimed that he was ready to start at once, whereas both his Panzer commanders admitted that

The 'White G' on the move: infantry of Guderian's group head south, mounted on a tank which bears their commander's initial

this was not possible. Guderian would not be ready until 15th August, and Hoth needed five days more than that, both stressing the need for new tank engines. Hitler reluctantly promised 300 for the whole of the eastern Front; Guderian rightly described this as totally inadequate, but Hitler refused to budge, and also refused to provide any new tanks, on the grounds that he needed them for equipping new Panzer formations being raised in Germany. Guderian re-emphasised the need to make good the tank losses, as the Red Army, despite its losses, still had a numerical superiority in tanks. Then Hitler made the statement – extraordinary in the context of his refusal to provide more tanks – that if he had believed Guderian's 1937 estimate of Soviet tank strength, he would not have started the war.

Guderian left the meeting determined to prepare the attack on Moscow whatever Hitler might intend; Hitler returned to his HQ at Rastenburg in east Prussia, in no doubt about his unpopularity with Army Group Centre.

His remark to Guderian about Red Army tank strength showed that he was beginning to have doubts of ultimate success, despite the victories so far gained. Many of his generals, too, were disquieted by the continued fierce resistance of the Red Army, while as their letters home showed, the troops themselves were becoming uneasy when faced with the apparently endless plains and the fact that no matter how many Russians they killed or captured, the next day found the Red Army apparently as vigorous as ever.

It had now become a question of nerve. OKH was disgruntled but still obedient; Army Group Centre, hypnotised by Moscow, was openly thwarting the directives it received from OKH; and Guderian was stubbornly trying to keep his Panzers in positions from which they could resume the eastward march. But while he was doing this, most of Panzer Group 3 was busily redeploying as ordered, to assist Army Group North in its move against Leningrad – its commander, Hoth, apparently being the only senior officer in Army Group Centre who still believed in doing what he was told.

The net result was a dispersion of effort and energy which furthered none of the objectives. While Guderian was finding reasons for not going back to Gomel to deal with the Soviet Fifth Army, and was submitting unacceptable plans to take Moscow, Army Group South stalled yet again in front of Kiev. The Commander-in-Chief of

German Sixth Army (Reichenau) observed that between him and Second Army of Army Group Centre was a gap of 150 miles. Sixty miles of this was covered by only one division (56th Infantry), while facing it were several divisions of Soviet Fifth Army. Reichenau's orders were to press ahead with a direct attack on Kiev, but with this threat at his back he objected to Rundstedt who, on 9th August, called off the offensive in the Kiev-Korosten area. Sixth Army resumed the defensive with its primary operational objective – Kiev – still unattained.

An analysis of the situation, made in OKW on the evening of the next day, showed the emergence of an uneasy

In the tracks of the Panzers: German infantry press southwards across the open steppe

compromise, designed to pacify the 'Moscow' faction without yielding to it. It was agreed that the main enemy forces were in front of Army Group Centre, and that the most important task was to destroy them and seize Moscow; but, it was argued, the forces facing the other two army Groups constituted a threat to Army Group Centre's flanks. Therefore the decisive attack on Moscow must be preceded by operations with limited aims against the forces in north and south.

On the assumption that destruction of these forces would take two weeks, a general offensive against Moscow, with infantry armies in the centre, and a Panzer Group on each flank, could begin at the end of August. The enemy would be forced to stand and fight with new and only partially trained forces on an incomplete defence line running roughly from Rzhev to Bryansk via Vyazma. If this plan were adopted, Army Groups North and South would have to deal with their enemies, for the time being, without assistance from Army Group Centre – though with complete assurance that once it had broken through the Soviet defences and begun the pursuit, it would be able to release some of its forces to assist them.

As for Army Group South, its Seventeenth Army was at present free for use, and should be employed in forcing the Dnieper between Kiev and Kremenchug, in order to break up the

The introduction by the Soviet Union of the T-34 marked the beginning of a new era in tank construction. It was heavily armed, fast and well armoured. *Crew:* four. *Weight:* 30.9 tons. *Armament:* one 76mm gun and two 7.62mm machine guns. *Ammunition:* 100 rounds of 76mm and 3,600 rounds of 7.62mm. *Armour:* 45mm front, sides and rear, 20mm roof and floor, and 52mm cast turret. *Maximum speed:* 35mph. *Range:* 190 miles

Klimenti Voroshilov KV-1. *Crew:* Five men. *Combat weight:* 43.5 tons. *Width:* 10 feet 9 inches. *Height:* 9 feet. *Length:* 22 feet 5 inches. *Maximum speed* 26 mph. *Armament:* One 76.2mm gun and three 7.62mm machine guns. *Armour:* front 75mm, side 60mm and turret side 75mm. *Engine:* One V-12 diesel motor, 550 hp

large Soviet forces forming up on the east bank. When the Dnieper line had been forced, part of Army Group South should turn north into the rear of the Soviet Fifth Army, so as to put paid to it once and for all.

On 12th August Hitler again emphasised that the pre-condition for all future operations was prior destruction of enemy forces on the flanks, in particular those on the right flank of Army Group Centre – that is, the Soviet Southwest Front. On the same day Budenny and Khrushchev wrote to Stalin in some uneasiness. They had observed that the German Second Army and Guderian's Panzers were making progress towards Gomel and Starodub, and had concluded that their object was to smash down behind Southwest Front and cut it off.

STAVKA, however, was just as hypnotised by Moscow as was Army Group Centre. Its assessment was that the movement which worried Budenny and Khrushchev was intended to exploit the large gap which had opened between Reserve and Central Fronts, and that the Germans would turn east into it, to break through at Bryansk and outflank Moscow from the south. Budenny had asked permission to withdraw Fifth Army and XXVII Independent Corps from the Korosten Fortified Zone, form a front to the north with them, and thus block the German drive across the rear of his Southwest Front. STAVKA refused, and instead ordered the formation of Bryansk Front, at first with responsibility only to fill the gap between Central and Reserve Fronts and prevent a German breakthrough to Moscow.

In the light of the information then available to it, STAVKA's decision was reasonable: as has already been said, Guderian tried to the last to keep the Moscow option open, and Hitler had not yet firmly ruled it out. Furthermore, the Soviet Fifth Army was in fact inhibiting Army Group South's advance on Kiev simply by hovering over the German rear; to withdraw it over the Desna, as Budenny wanted to do, would have relieved the Germans of one of their worst headaches, and this was a good reason for keeping it where it was. But the decision, reasonable though it seemed, turned out to be a disastrous mistake, for the Germans were at last making up their minds what to do. And STAVKA's guess – that Moscow would be the target – was wrong.

On 15th August Hitler abandoned the pretence that Army Group Centre could continue its offensive on Moscow with infantry only, and ordered a complete halt to its advance. Instead it was to organise a defence which the Soviets could not encircle, could be held without substantial air support and would be economical in its use of infantry. Three days later Brauchitsch made a last desperate plea for the Moscow operation. He pointed out that the onset of winter in the Moscow area could be expected in mid-October, five weeks earlier than in the Ukraine, and argued that concentration on Moscow would make its capture possible before the bad weather set in, thus freeing forces for use in the south where the campaigning season was longer.

In reply, Hitler rejected Brauchitsch's arguments out of hand, and set out his own views. He repeated his contention that the Panzer columns, by outstripping the infantry and operating too independently, had produced only partial encirclements from which large numbers of the enemy had been able to escape. His rejection of OKW's proposals for a Moscow operation was formalised as an unnumbered Directive, issued on 21st August, which laid down, in clear and unambiguous terms, the tasks to be fulfilled before the onset of winter. It stated that the taking of Moscow before the winter was not a primary objective. The first priorities were, in the south the taking of the Crimea and the industrial and coal area of the Donets basin, together with the cutting of the supply routes for

Caucasus oil, and in the north to invest Leningrad and establish contact with the Finns.

As for Army Group Centre, it must join Army Group South in a concentric operation against the Soviet Fifth Army, with the objective of not merely driving it back across the Dnieper (as would be the case if Sixth Army alone conducted the operation), but of destroying it, so as to give Army Group South the necessary security for its further operations across the Dnieper and into the Donets basin. Capture of the Crimea was of extreme importance for safeguarding oil supplies from Roumania, since Soviet bombers could attack the Ploesti oilfields from Crimean air bases.

This, then, was the vital decision. The idea of actually capturing Leningrad was quietly abandoned, and an advance on Moscow was ruled out for the time being. Soviet Fifth Army was to be disposed of once and for all, and the main effort was to be in the Ukraine. Nothing could be plainer.

Yet even now there was to be one last attempt to keep the Moscow operation alive. On 23rd August, a conference was held at HQ Army Group Centre, at which Halder outlined the provisions of the directive. There was then a long discussion of ways in which the Führer's mind might be changed, and it was finally decided that Guderian should go back to Hitler's HQ with Halder. They left that afternoon, landing at Lötzen (the nearest airfield to Rastenburg) at dusk.

Guderian reported immediately to Brauchitsch, who categorically forbade him to reopen the question of Moscow with Hitler. But Guderian was by now not to be stopped by anyone, and in reporting on the state of his Panzer group he contrived to lead the conversation around so that Hitler himself introduced the subject. The Panzer General repeated all the arguments for an attack on the Soviet capital, adding that the troops were expecting it, and were prepared for it.

Army Group Centre was poised ready for it, and a long detour into the south would cause heavy additional wear and tear, as well as loss of time.

Hitler heard him out without challenging any of his statements, even though Guderian's claim that Army Group Centre was poised for an attack on Moscow was particularly dubious, as both Panzer groups were short of engines and tanks, and neither was suitably deployed. Hoth's tanks were away assisting Army Group North, and Guderian's partly engaged in a southward move around Starodub. But Hitler was not to be moved; the Moscow offensive was absolutely excluded until the operation in the south had been brought to a successful conclusion.

Guderian bowed to the inevitable, and suggested that his whole Panzer group, rather than part of it, be committed to the southern operation to ensure success. Hitler agreed, and Guderian returned at once to Army Group Centre. The next morning he broke the news to Halder, and an angry scene ensued. But there could be no more argument. Kiev was the objective.

It has already been said that the Military Council of Soviet Southwest Front had become uneasy as early as 12th August. On 18th August General Zhukov, commanding Reserve Front before Moscow, noticed that the Germans facing him had become less active. On discovering that the same was true on the adjacent Central Front, he began considering what this portended. He was contemplating a fluid situation and his information was incomplete. However he concluded that the Germans might be regrouping for a drive southwards across the rear of Kiev and Southwest Front, and wrote to STAVKA on 18th August, indicating the possibility and suggesting that a strong force be established in the Bryansk area, with the aim of driving in Guderian's flank as he moved across in front of them. STAVKA replied, accepting his assess-

Introduced late in 1940, the 50mm PAK (Panzer Abwehrkanone – anti-tank gun) Model 38 remained in service throughout the war, though augmented by heavier weapons in later years. *Weight:* 2,174lbs. *Range:* 2,650m with HE shell *Rate of fire:* twelve rounds per minute. Using standard armour piercing shell, it could penetrate 78mm of armour at 500 yards. With tungsten-cored shot, this was improved to 120mm at the same range

The 10.5cm leFH (leicht Feld Haubitze – light field howitzer) Model 18M was a standard Model 18 with a muzzle brake added and the recoil mechanism adjusted in order to fire a speeded long-range shell. *Weight:* 1,985kg. *Range:* normal shell, 10,675m; special shell, 12,850m. Both shells weighed 32.5lbs but a special cartridge fired the long-range shell. In addition, a wide range of smoke, star, anti-tank, and even propaganda-filled shells were provided

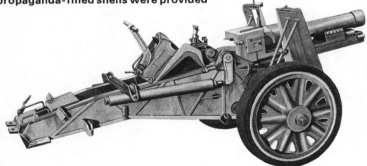

The 15cm sIG (schweres Infanterie Geschutz – heavy infantry gun) Model 33 was developed by Rheinmettal in 1927 and remained in use until 1945 with infantry cannon companies of Grenadier and Panzer-Grenadier regiments. *Weight:* 1,700kg. *Range:* 5,150 yards. *Shell weight:* 83lb HE, 85lb Smoke, 55lb Hollow charge anti-tank

ment, and claiming that it had already foreseen the danger and had, for this reason, established Bryansk Front a few days before. It is doubtful whether this was true. The front commander, General Yeremenko, subsequently claimed that his orders were to guard against a breakthrough towards Moscow, and this may well have been his initial directive.

On 19th August STAVKA belatedly granted Budenny's request for permission to withdraw all his forces beyond the Dnieper, ordering only that Thirty-seventh Army remain in Kiev. The withdrawn forces (Fifth Army and a new Fortieth, made up of remnants of other armies) were to form line to the north, defending Chernigov, Konotop and Kharkov. So far, matters were moving along the right lines: the German intentions had been divined even before they were finalised, and dispositions made to meet Guderian both frontally and on his left flank. But this also meant that Budenny's bolt was shot; his units were thoroughly battered and combat-weary, and he had no reserves left for Southwest Front. Everything now depended on Yeremenko.

On 24th August, Stalin spoke to Yeremenko by telephone, offering him two more tank brigades, several tank battalions, some Katyusha rocket batteries, and several air force regiments – 'if you promise to beat that scoundrel Guderian'. He also offered another army (the Twenty-first) formed from the tattered Third and Twenty-first Armies of the Central Front, and this, too, Yeremenko accepted. The Chief of General Staff, Marshal Shaposhnikov, then came on the line, reiterating the belief that Guderian might turn through a right-angle and head north of Bryansk, making for Moscow. Thus he introduced a fatal ambiguity into Yeremenko's instructions, by inserting

Beginning of the end: first of the hundreds of thousands of Russians taken in the Kiev pocket

the fear that Bryansk Front might be left high and dry with neither its original nor its second mission accomplished. In an attempt to cover both contingencies, Yeremenko held back his strongest force, the Fiftieth Army, to protect the routes to Moscow, and Shaposhnikov's anxious caution thus prejudiced the success of the counteroffensive a week before it began.

Nevertheless, the forces available to Yeremenko for his westward thrust were formidable. Central Front had been disbanded on 25th August, and its forces subordinated to him, giving him two armies (Thirteenth and Twenty-first) plus the entire High Command Reserve of aircraft and the air support forces of Central and Reserve Fronts to add to those of his own front. So emaciated was the Red Air Force as a result of its earlier losses that even this force totalled only 464 aircraft, half of which were bombers. STAVKA could do little more now. They, too, had no more reserves to spare.

The Soviet offensive began on 30th August, when Yeremenko's troops moved forward to bite at Guderian's flanking force, the XLVII Mechanised Corps. Despite all their efforts, they made little impression, and further north and west the German Second Army began to push back Yeremenko's Twenty-first Army. The Twenty-first recoiled back on to the small and hurriedly formed Thirtieth Army of Southwest Front, which soon broke and began retreating towards the southeast. Thus the Twenty-first Army was soon completely cut off from the rest of Bryansk Front, having been deeply penetrated on both sides – by the German Second Army to the west of it, and by Guderian's Panzers to its east. It began to withdraw hastily to the southeast, completely out of contact with the High Command, and with German troops pouring into the gaps on each side of it.

STAVKA had laid too heavy a task on Bryansk Front, and having done so, was reluctant to believe that

Yeremenko could not pull it off. On 2nd September Stalin wrote petulantly to him: 'STAVKA is still not satisfied with your work . . . You have rattled the enemy just a little, but you haven't succeeded in driving him off his positions. Guderian and all his group must be smashed to pieces. Until this is done, all that you say about successes is worthless. We are waiting for you to report that you have defeated Guderian's group'.

When it became clear that the Yeremenko counteroffensive was not succeeding, STAVKA's reaction was not to liquidate the undertaking but to pour more forces into it from other sections of the line. Shaposhnikov ordered Budenny to hand over his II Cavalry Corps, and this, for the old revolutionary, was the last straw. On 10th September he spoke to Shaposhnikov by radio, pointing out that this was his only reserve for Southern Front on the whole Dnepropetrovsk-Kharkov line, a distance of about 125 miles, and saying: 'I ask you to turn your attention to what Yeremenko's doing. He was supposed to stop this enemy group, but nothing's come of it.' Shaposhnikov, however, insisted, and the exasperated Budenny said: 'All right . . . the order to move will be issued right away. Please report my views to the Supreme Commander [Stalin], especially about the operations of Bryansk Front.'

The following day, the Military Council of Southwest Front, Budenny, Khrushchev, and Pokrovsky, addressed themselves directly to Stalin. They formally requested permission to withdraw their forces to the east, pointing out that the entire Southwest Front was now in serious danger of encirclement from the direction of Novgorod Severski (Guderian's starting point) and Kremenchug (where Kleist's Panzer Group 1 and German Seventeenth Army had established a bridgehead over the Dnieper, from which Kleist was hastening north to link up with Guderian). They stated that they had already asked Shaposhnikov for permission to withdraw, and that he had refused, ordering them instead to move two of Twenty-sixth Army's divisions to block Guderian between Bakhmach and Konotop. Clearly they felt that Shaposhnikov was losing his grip under pressure of events – to carry out this order would have left the one remaining division of Twenty-sixth Army (whose losses in action had reduced it to less than 10,000 men) to guard one hundred miles of the Dnieper against German forces which outnumbered it by more than six to one.

Stalin at once contacted the Commander of Southwest Front, Colonel-General Kirponos, and sought his views. Kirponos said firmly that his Front should be withdrawn from the Kiev salient to the line of the River Psel, some 150 miles to the east. But this Stalin categorically rejected. He ordered Kirponos to hold Kiev at whatever cost, and to move in all forces that could be brought there. Since Budenny was heading a consensus for withdrawal, Stalin dismissed him, appointing in his place Marshal Timoshenko, so far the most successful of the older generation of Soviet soldiers. But by now it was too late to save the situation. The gap between Guderian and Kleist was less than sixty miles wide, and the Panzer groups were moving towards each other far faster than the encircled Soviet forces could move towards the shrinking corridor. Even if they started at once, most of them would probably not get through. Yet Shaposhnikov, presumably obeying Stalin's orders, would still not allow them to move.

Guderian, travelling with 3rd Panzer Division at the head of Panzer Group 2, met Kleist's tanks at Lokhvitsa on 15th September. Four Soviet Armies, the Fifth, Twenty-first, Twenty-sixth and Thirty-seventh, were trapped. Southwest Front began to fall apart, and its communications were soon in such a state of chaos that Timoshenko the next day ordered his forces east of the German cordon to hold open the

corridor to the east, unaware that there was now no corridor left. He and Khrushchev decided to abandon Kiev in defiance of Stalin's order, but Kirponos insisted on orders from STAVKA, so more valuable time was lost.

While Stalin and Shaposhnikov were debating the question in Moscow, the German ring was hardening. Only at 2340 hours on the following day (17th September) did STAVKA authorise the abandonment of Kiev. Two nights which could have been used for extricating troops (movement by day was almost impossible, so complete by now was the German air superiority) had been wasted, and what would in any case have been a major defeat was turned by Stalin's vacillation into a catastrophe. In the middle of the night of 17th–18th September, Kirponos ordered all his armies to fight their way out of the cauldron.

But the breakthrough was doomed to failure. Thirty-seventh Army, defending the city area of Kiev itself, had already lost contact with Front HQ, never received the order to break out, and surrendered in the city after fighting on for two days. Within a few hours Kirponos had lost contact with his other three armies, Fifth, Twenty-first and Twenty-sixth, and with STAVKA. Southwest Front now existed only in name; the only part of it still under Kirponos's command was the 289th Rifle Division, to which he and his staff had attached themselves, but even this became dispersed in the course of the night, and by the time it reached Gorodishche only some 3,000 men were left. These were split into several detachments, but only a handful escaped. They did not include any of the Military Council of Southwest Front; all three (Kirponos, Burmistenko and Tupikov) had been killed.

On the eastern side of the cauldron, the Red Army manned its positions and looked west, with dwindling hopes for some sign of the encircled armies. Soon small groups began to arrive.

Major-General Bagramyan, who had taken the order to retreat to Kirponos, came through with fifty men. General Kuznetsov, commanding Twenty-first Army, brought out his survivors in good order, but they numbered only 500. General Kostenko brought out only a few men of his Twenty-sixth Army. Brigade Commander Borisov came out with 4,000 cavalrymen. Senior Battalion Commissar Gorban led out fifty-two signallers from the front staff. And there were other detachments, but none were large.

Behind them, dead or imprisoned, they left over 500,000 men – the precise number is disputed, and Army Group South claimed 665,000 prisoners alone, while Soviet sources admit to 527,000 dead, captured or missing. Even the lower figure comprised more than

An army goes into captivity. Thousands of defeated Russian soldiers being herded across the vast plains

two-thirds of the strength of South-west Front at the beginning of the war, a mere three months previously. In terms of numbers lost it was the biggest catastrophe in Russian history, and for Guderian (much though he would have preferred to go to Moscow), it was a complete justi-fication of his concept of armoured warfare. Soon he would be able to test his ideas against Moscow itself, and see whether the Soviet preoccupation with that city, which had so harmed

their assessments of other threats, would make them capable of defending it more effectively than they had defended Kiev.

But this would be the biggest test of all. And the campaigning season was beginning to run out. Much time had been lost in the south, and more would be lost while Guderian's tanks made their way back to the north, made good the wear and tear of the dash to Lokhvitsa, and regrouped to seize the greatest prize of all – Moscow.

The battle
for the capital

The regrouping necessary for the final assault on Moscow was large, as three Panzer Groups, 2 (Guderian) 3 (Hoth) and 4 (Hoeppner) were to be used. Of these only Hoth's was already in position, as Hoeppner's had to be transferred from the Leningrad Front (this was done during the second half of September), and Guderian's had to make its way back from the Ukraine.

The Directive for Operation 'Typhoon' was issued on 16th September. It envisaged another Cannae as large as that then being accomplished in the Ukraine, in which most of two Soviet Army Groups, Konev's Western and Yeremenko's Bryansk Fronts, would be encircled and destroyed in the opening stage – the two 'cauldron' battles of Vyazma and Bryansk. The road to Moscow would lie open, or so it was hoped, and it would be out-flanked to north and south in a gigantic pincer movement closing well to the east. Bock had available to him sixty-eight divisions, fourteen Panzer, eight motorised and forty-six infantry, in three Panzer groups and three armies. He was faced by three Soviet Fronts, Western with six armies, Bryansk with three armies and an operational group, and Reserve Front with six armies, two of which were deployed alongside Western Front while the other four were in second echelon behind it. However each Soviet army was equivalent in size only to a German army corps, and was inferior to it in firepower, more particularly because half the artillery had been withdrawn from the divisions to form a High Command Artillery Reserve, while German air support was superior both in number and in quality.

The 'Typhoon' operation began on 30th September, when Panzer Group 2 was launched northeastwards towards Orel, from where it would drive north

After the disasters of Smolensk, Uman, and Kiev, Zhukov prepares for the decisive battle: the defence of Moscow

behind Yeremenko's troops. On 2nd October the remainder of the Army Group, as the OKH Operations Report put it, 'went over to the offensive in beautiful autumn weather. The attack took the enemy by surprise along the entire front'.

Success at first was brilliant. Guderian's tanks swept into Orel before the city had an inkling of their approach. They found the trams still running, and were cheered by civilians who took them for Soviet reinforcements. Panzer Groups 3 and 4 further north fared equally well, and by 7th October, a mere five days after the launching of the main offensive, Army Group Centre had the bulk of Konev's forces, Sixteenth, Nineteenth and Twentieth Armies and General Boldin's army-sized Operational Group, west of Vyazma, while in another pocket northeast of Bryansk Yeremenko's three armies (Third, Thirteenth and Fiftieth) were trapped, along with the Twenty-fourth and Thirty-second Armies of the Reserve Front. Altogether eighty-one Soviet divisions were encircled in the Vyazma-Bryansk pockets, and the entire Soviet defensive front before Moscow was on the verge of collapse.

The encirclement was less tight than it had been at Kiev, and the 'beautiful autumn weather' mentioned by OKH did not last long. By the 6th it had been succeeded by the 'rasputitsa', the season of bad roads, which occurs twice a year in Russia, when the snow melts in the spring and when the autumn rains fall. Since most of the roads were, and still are, unsurfaced, the rasputitsa turns them into quagmire, and so it happened in October 1941. The German drive slowed down, and it became almost impossible to maintain progress. The mud, naturally, affected Soviet operations too. Yeremenko, trapped in the Bryansk pocket with his troops, personally led the repulse of a German attack on his headquarters, then ordered his armies to turn their front through 180 degrees and fight their way out to the east. In their flight they found the mud almost as much of a hindrance as the Germans, although by confining the Germans to a handful of roads it made the Soviet escape through marshes and forests that much easier. Even so, Bryansk Front had to fight its way through five German positions, and when Yeremenko's troops emerged into Soviet-held territory few of his divisions had as many as 3,000 men left, of a nominal war establishment of 14,300. Zhukov, in the account which follows, refers caustically to German complaints about the mud, and points out that it hindered the building of defensive positions, mostly by women from Moscow. This, too, is a valid point, and it would be senseless to ignore the difficulties which the *rasputitsa* presented to the Soviet side in its frantic attempts to shore up the collapsing front. Nevertheless, in so far as the mud slowed up the Panzer forces, it was a lesser hindrance to the Russians than to the Germans, as it helped them to gain time. Having gained that time, the Soviet forces, under Zhukov's leadership, made good use of it. He himself says that the most critical period of the Moscow battle was the few days following 18th October when, following the closing of the Vyazma and Bryansk pockets 'the approaches to Moscow were in fact not covered'. During that period the *rasputitsa* was at its worst, ending only at the beginning of November when the frosts hardened the ground.

Marshal Zhukov has some harsh criticisms to make of the way in which Konev and Yeremenko allowed their forces to be trapped and almost annihilated, and it was probably in the Battle of Moscow that he laid the foundations for the hearty dislike which both these distinguished Marshals have displayed towards him ever since. There is, no doubt, a great deal of justice in what he says; but it must be borne in mind that we do not know, because the Soviet Union has not chosen to tell us, what instruc-

tions they had received from the STAVKA, of which Zhukov even at that time was a leading member. If they had been ordered to stand fast, or were given permission to withdraw only when it was too late to do so, they would be no more to blame than Kirponos, who paid for Stalin's stubbornness with his life and most of his army group. Certainly Stalin, although he replaced Konev with Zhukov, retained him as Deputy Commander of Western Front, and within a few weeks gave him command of a new army group, Kalinin Front. Yeremenko was wounded during the escape from Bryansk, and remained in hospital for some weeks. Stalin visited him there (a rare honour, for he did not often leave the Kremlin), and expressed approval of Bryansk Front's performance. Furthermore, in July 1942, when Yeremenko was recovering from yet another wound, he appointed him to the very crucial post of Commander of the army group defending Stalingrad. These incidents hardly suggest that Stalin regarded either man as responsible through incompetence for the loss of most of their troops at Vyazma and Bryansk, but rather that he considered STAVKA (and therefore himself) as in large part to blame. Zhukov, as his record perhaps entitles him to do, sets a very high standard in his evaluation of generalship, and it is clear from his own writings that the Battle of Moscow was the one that meant most to him. It was the first time he had ever handled so large a body of men, about a million. It was the one in which failure on his part could bring the entire state crashing down almost at once; and it was fought over the terrain most familiar to him, because here he had spent the whole of his childhood. From the accounts of others it would seem that during this battle he was at his most abusive, sarcastic, and demanding. The late Marshal Rokossovsky, himself a general of brilliance and, unlike Zhukov, a tolerant and genial man,

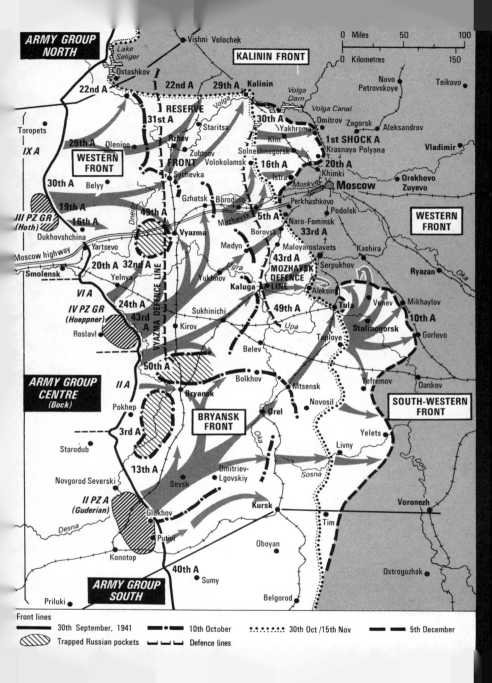

ARMY GROUP NORTH

Vishni Volochek

KALININ FRONT

Lake Seliger

Ostashkov

Toropets

22nd A

22nd A   29th A   Kalinin

IX A

RESERVE
31st A

29th A   Olenino

WESTERN
FRONT

Rzhev   Staritsa

Zubtsov

30th A   Belyy

Sychevka   Volokolamsk

FRONT
49th A

Gzhatsk   Borodino

III PZ GR
(Hoth)

19th A

16th A

Dukhovshchina

Yartsevo

Moscow highway

Smolensk

20th A   32nd A

Yelnya

Yelnya

VI A

24th A

IV PZ GR
(Hoeppner)

Roslavl

43rd
A

Novo
Petrovskoye   Teikovo

Volga
Dam

Volga Canal

30th A   Dmitrov   Zagorsk
Yakhroma   Aleksandrov

Klin   1st SHOCK A
Solnechnogorsk   Krasnaya Polyana

16th A   20th A
Istra   Khimki

Moskva'   Moscow

Perkhushkovo   Podolsk

Mozhaysk   5th A'   Naro-Fominsk

Borovsk   33rd A

Medyn   Maloyaroslavets

Vyazma

Vladimir

Orekhovo
Zuyevo

WESTERN
FRONT

Kashira

Serpukhov

Ryazan

Oka

43rd A
MOZHAYSK
DEFENCE
LINE

Yukhnov

Kaluga

Aleksin

Sukhinichi

Kirov

Tula

Venev   Mikhaylov

Stalinogorsk

10th A

Gorlovo

Teploye

Belev

Upa

ARMY GROUP
CENTRE
(Bock)

50th A

II A

Pokhep

Bryansk

Bolkhov

Mtsensk

Yefremov   Dankov

3rd A

Starodub

13th A

Novosil

Orel

SOUTH-WESTERN
FRONT

BRYANSK
FRONT

Oka

Livny

Yelets

Voronezh

Novgorod Severski

II PZ A
(Guderian)

Glukhov

Dmitriev-
Lgovskiy

Sevsk

Sosna

Don

Desna

Putivl

Kursk

Tim

Ostrogozhsk

Konotop

40th A

Oboyan

ARMY GROUP
SOUTH

Sumy

Priluki

Belgorod

Miles   50   100

Kilometres   150

Front lines

———— 30th September, 1941   ▬•▬•▬ 10th October   •••••••• 30th Oct /15th Nov   ▬ ▬ ▬ 5th December

▨▨ Trapped Russian pockets   ⌐ ⌐ ⌐ Defence lines

popular with his colleagues, and popular with his troops too because of his economy in expenditure of their lives, said of Zhukov 'in the heat of the battle of Moscow, Zhukov was sometimes more sharp than was justified'. This should be borne in mind when reading Zhukov's remarks about the Vyazma-Bryansk encirclements, and the shortcomings of the army group commanders.

Marshal Zhukov's account of the circumstances in which he took charge of the defence of Moscow, and of the fighting which preceded the Soviet counteroffensive of December, here follows.

The Battle for the Capital
by Marshal G K Zhukov
The beginning of October 1941 found me in Leningrad where I was commanding the forces of Leningrad Front (Zhukov, then an Army General, had been appointed to his post by Stalin at the beginning of September, to succeed Marshal Voroshilov). But

Above: On a Moscow roof, AA machine-gunners keep watch for the Luftwaffe. *Right:* The Soviet capital under German air attack

it is not my mission to talk now about what the Nazi plunderers had planned for the city which carries the name of the great Lenin, or of the September battles of Leningrad Front.

In October the enemy undertook an offensive which he planned would end with the capture of our Motherland's capital.

At the beginning of the German offensive on the Moscow axis three Fronts (Western, Reserve and Bryansk) were defending the distant approaches to Moscow.

Altogether at the end of September the combat forces of Western, Reserve and Bryansk Fronts comprised about 800,000 men, with 770 tanks and 9,150 guns, the Western Front having more men and weapons than the others.

The German Army Group Centre, as

we now know, comprised more than 1,000,000 men, 1,700 tanks and assault guns and more than 19,000 guns and mortars, supported by *Luftflotte* 2, commanded by Field-Marshal Kesselring. In a directive of 16th September Hitler set Army Group Centre the assignment of breaking through the Soviet defence, encircling and destroying the main forces of the Western, Reserve and Bryansk Fronts, and then pursuing the remnants of them, to encircle Moscow from south and north and capture it.

On 30th September 1941 the enemy began an offensive against Bryansk Front, and on 2nd October struck hard at the Western and Reserve Fronts. Especially strong blows followed from north of Dukhovschchina and east of Roslavl, against the Thirtieth and Nineteenth Armies of the Western Front and the Forty-third Army of Reserve Front. The Germans succeeded in breaking through our defence and enemy assault groups advanced at a headlong pace, outflanking the entire Vyazma group of forces of the Western and Reserve Fronts from south and north.

An exceedingly serious situation arose on Bryansk Front too, where the Third and Thirteenth Armies were under threat of encirclement. Without meeting any particular resistance, Guderian's army headed part of its forces towards Orel, where Bryansk Front had no forces with which to beat them back. On 3rd October the enemy captured Orel. Bryansk Front was cut to pieces: its forces retreated with heavy losses to the east and south-east, and in consequence a dangerous situation arose on the Tula axis.

The commander of the Western Front, Colonel-General Konev, ordered Lieutenant-General IV Boldin's Operational Group to mount a counter-attack against the enemy force which was outflanking from the north, but it was a failure, and by the evening of 6th October a substantial part of the

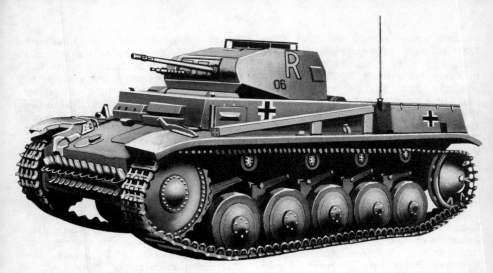

Panzerkampfwagen Pzkpfw-II
The Pzkpfw-II comprised the majority of the tanks of the German armoured
regiments at the outbreak of war in 1939. It was essentially a lightly-armed
scout tank. *Weight:* 10 tons. *Speed:* 30 mph. *Crew:* three. *Armour:* 15mm (max).
Armament: one 20mm cannon, one 7.92mm machine-gun

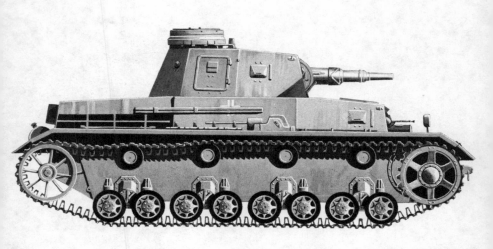

The Hanomag Sd Kfz 251 provided light battlefield support for the infantry. The vehicle was underpowered and difficult to steer. *Weight:* about 8.5 tons. *Armament:* one 37mm cannon and one 7.92mm machine gun. *Armour:* 12mm front and 7mm rest. *Maximum speed:* 34mph. *Range:* 200 miles. *Engine:* Maybach HL 42 6-cylinder 4.2 litre watercooled engine developing 100bhp

Panzerkampfwagen Pzkpfw-IIIF
The standard medium tank of the German Panzer divisions at the time of the German onslaught on Russia. *Weight:* 20 tons. *Speed:* 24mph. *Crew:* five. *Armour:* 30mm. *Armament:* one 50mm gun, two 7.92mm machine-guns

Western Front's forces (units of Lieutenant-General MF Lukin's Nineteenth Army, of Lieutenant-General KK Rokossovsky's Sixteenth Army, of Lieutenant-General FA Yershakov's Twentieth Army, and of General Boldin's Operational Group) and Reserve Front (Major-General SV Vishnevsky's Thirty-second Army, and Major-General KI Rakutin's Twenty-fourth Army) were surrounded in the area west of Vyazma.

That evening (6th October) the Supreme Commander, J V Stalin, telephoned me and asked how things were at Leningrad. I reported that the enemy had ceased attacking, and that prisoners said German losses had been heavy and the offensive had been abandoned. The city was being bombarded by artillery and aircraft, but our air reconnaissance had established that large scale movement of mechanised and tank columns from the Leningrad area to the south was under way. Clearly the German High Command was transferring these forces to the Moscow axis.

Stalin listened to my report, was silent for a moment, and then said that we were in serious trouble on the Moscow axis, especially on the Western Front.

'Leave your Chief of Staff, General Khozin, behind you as Acting Commander of Leningrad Front, and fly to Moscow,' he ordered. I passed on the Supreme Commander's order to Khozin, said goodbye to the members of the Military Council, and flew to Moscow. On 7th October, as darkness was falling, I landed at the central airfield, and made my way to the Kremlin.

Stalin was in his apartment. He was not well – he had a cold. He greeted me with a nod of his head, then pointed to the map and said: 'Here, look. A very serious situation has arisen, but I can't get a detailed report on how things really are on the Western Front.' And he suggested to me that I should go at once to its headquarters and forces, take very careful account of the situation, and then telephone him at any time of the night. 'I'll be waiting,' he said, and that was how the conversation ended.

Within fifteen minutes I was with the Chief of General Staff, getting a map from him and acquainting myself with the situation, even if only in general terms. Marshal Shaposhnikov looked very overtired. As he greeted me he said that the Supreme Commander had already telephoned him and told him to give me a map of the Western axis, 'The map will be here shortly. The headquarters of the Western Front are where the headquarters of Reserve Front were in August, when you were conducting the operations against the Yelnya salient.'

While telling me about the serious situation at the fronts, he added that the work of building defence positions on the Mozhaysk line and the near approaches to Moscow was not yet finished, and there were as yet hardly any troops there. The State Defence Committee, the Central Committee of the Party, and the Supreme High Command were taking steps to stop the enemy offensive. It was essential to put troops at once into the defensive lines, above all into the Mozhaysk line. Formations and units from STAVKA Reserve and neighbouring fronts had begun redeploying to that line on the previous night (6th–7th October).

At 2.30 am on the night of 7th-8th October I telephoned Stalin, who was still working. When I had reported the situation on the Western Front I said: 'The chief danger now is that there is practically nothing covering the roads to Moscow, and the weak *ad hoc* units deployed in the Mozhaysk line give no guarantee against a breakthrough to Moscow by German Panzer forces. Troops must be brought into the Mozhaysk defence line as quickly as possible, from wherever they can be got.'

Stalin asked, 'Where now are the Sixteenth, Nineteenth, Twentieth

Armies and Boldin's group of the Western Front, Twenty-fourth and Thirty-second Armies of Reserve Front?'

'Encircled, north and northwest of Vyazma.'

'What do you intend to do?'

'I'm going to see Budenny . . .'

'Do you know where his headquarters are now?'

'No I don't. I'll look around in the Maloyaroslavets area.'

'All right, go to Budenny and telephone from there.'

A fine drizzle was falling, thick mist was hovering over the ground, and visibility was bad. At dawn on 8th October, as we approached the junction at Obninskoye (105 kilometres from Moscow) we saw two signallers laying a cable from the side of a bridge over the River Protva. When I asked them to where they were laying this communications line, I received a very unforthcoming answer. 'We are laying it to where we've been ordered,'

Vyazma/Bryansk: the Red Army takes another mauling

answered a very large soldier in a voice full of cold. It was clear that they were old soldiers with no intention of answering questions from persons whom they did not know. I had to identify myself and tell them that I was looking for Marshal Budenny's Reserve Front Headquarters. The same immense signaller explained that we had already passed the Front Headquarters, and now would have to turn back into the forest to the heights on the left of the bridge, and ask the guard the way from there.

Within ten minutes I was in the room of Army Commissar 1st Rank L Z Mekhlis, with whom was the Chief of Staff, Major-General A F Anisov. Mekhlis was giving somebody a severe dressing-down over the telephone, and after he had put the instrument down, he asked me what I was doing there. I

85

explained that I had come on Stalin's order as a member of STAVKA, to find out what was happening, and that I in my turn, would be interested to know where his Commander was. He explained that Budenny had been with Forty-third Army on the previous day, but that nobody knew where he was now, and the staff were worried that something might have happened to him. Signals officers had been sent out to find him, but had not yet returned. Neither Mekhlis nor Anisov could tell me anything definite about the state of Reserve Front's forces, or about the enemy.

'Well, you see what a state we are in,' said Mekhlis, 'I am collecting the stragglers together. We'll re-arm them at assembly points, and form new units out of them.'

I had to go on further towards Yukhnov, via Maloyaroslavets and Medyn, hoping to clarify the situation more quickly on the spot. As I passed the Protva and Obinskoye my childhood and youth came back unbidden. It was from this junction that my mother had sent me as a twelve year old boy, to relatives in Moscow to learn the trade of a tanner. Four years later, already qualified at it, I frequently came from Moscow to the village and my parents. I knew all the ground around Maloyaroslavets well, as I had been all over it in my younger days. Only ten kilometres from Obinskoye where the headquarters of Reserve Front now stood, was the village of Strelkovka, where I was born and passed the whole of my childhood; my mother and my sister with her four children were still living there. What would happen to them I thought, if the Nazis arrived there? Would they find out that these are the mother, sister and nephews of General Zhukov? And if they did . . . Three days later an adjutant whom I had sent to fetch them, took them from the village to my apartment in Moscow.

Here was Maloyaroslavets already. All the way to the town centre we met not a single living soul. The town seemed to have died. But outside the building of the Regional Executive Committee stood two light vehicles. In the cab of one was a driver, asleep. We woke him up; he said that this was Budenny's machine, and that Budenny himself had already been inside the Regional Executive Committee building for three hours.

As I entered the building I saw Budenny, and we greeted each other warmly. It was apparent that he had been through a great deal in those tragic days.

When he learnt that I had visited the Western Front's Headquarters, Budenny explained that he himself had had no means of contacting Konev for more than two days, while during his visit to Forty-third Army his own Front's Headquarters had moved, and he did not know where they had settled.

I told Budenny that his headquarters were 105 kilometres from Moscow, behind the railway bridge over the River Protva, and that they were waiting for him there. I also told him that things were very bad at Western Front, a large part of whose forces had been surrounded.

'It's no better with us,' observed Budenny in reply. 'Twenty-fourth and Thirty-second Armies are cut off, and there is no defensive front. Yesterday I myself very nearly fell into enemy hands between Yukhnov and Vyazma. Large enemy tank and motorised columns were heading towards Vyazma, obviously aiming to outflank the town from the east.'

'Who holds Yukhnov?'

'I don't know now. There was a small unit deployed and up to two regiments of infantry, with no artillery, on the Ugra River. I think Yukhnov is in enemy hands.'

'Well, who's covering the road from Yukhnov to Maloyaroslavets?'

'When I went there,' said Budenny, 'I met nobody except three policemen in Medyn.'

We agreed that Budenny would go

The *rasputitsa*: Russia's roads dissolve in mud . . .

... and the *Blitzkrieg* squelches to an ignominious halt

at once to his Front Headquarters and report the state of affairs to STAVKA from there, while I would go on to the Yukhnov area and then to Kaluga.

Very soon after our car had left Medyn for Yukhnov, our way was blocked where the road passed through a wood by armed Red Army men in overalls and tank men's helmets. One of them approached, warned us that it was not possible to go further, and asked me to identify myself. When I had done so I asked in my turn where their unit was. It turned out that it was nearby, in the wood, one hundred metres away, and was the headquarters of a tank brigade.

I was glad to hear this and asked them to take me to the headquarters. When we had entered the wood, a tall tank man in blue overalls, with goggles on top of his cap, rose from a small tree stump where he was sitting and came to meet us. Something about him struck me at once as familiar.

'Commander of Tank Brigade of STAVKA Reserve, Colonel Troitsky reporting.'

So that was who it was! I knew Troitsky well from Khalkhin Gol. In 1939 he had been Chief of Staff of the 11th Tank Brigade, and it was this very brigade which under the command of Hero of the Soviet Union Yakovlev had defeated the 23rd Infantry Division, part of the Japanese Imperial Guard, at Bain-tsagan mountain.

After we had greeted each other briefly we got down to business. Colonel Troitsky reported that the enemy was occupying Yukhnov, and that German forward units had seized the bridge over the Ugra river. A patrol sent by Troitsky towards Kaluga had established that there were no Germans there yet, but that fierce fighting was already going on near the town, where the 5th Guards Rifle Division and some retreating units of Forty-third Army were in action. As to Troitsky's own brigade, which was part of the STAVKA Reserve, it had

already been where I found it for two days, but had received no orders from anyone.

I ordered Troitsky to send signals officers to Headquarters, Reserve Front, at the Obninskoye railway halt, to tell Budenny about the situation, to deploy part of the brigade on the terrain in front and to organise a defence to cover the Medyn axis. I also ordered the Colonel to notify the General Staff, through Headquarters Reserve Front, of the orders I had given him, and to tell them that I had gone to Kaluga, to the 5th Guards Rifle Division. Troitsky and I said goodbye to each other as old comrades in arms.

On 9th October the Chief of Reserve Front Headquarters sought me out and handed me a telephone message from the Chief of the General Staff, Marshal Shaposhnikov. It said – 'The Supreme Commander has ordered you to go to Headquarters Western Front. You are appointed Commander of the Western Front.'

Thus ended my two day journey to the troops in my capacity as a member of STAVKA of the Supreme High Command, carrying out the Supreme Commander's assignment to find out what was happening. Early on the morning of 10th October I arrived in the area two or three miles northwest of Mozhaysk, where Headquarters Western Front were located. It turned out that a Commission from the State Defence Committee consisting of KE Voroshilov, GM Malenkov, VM Molotov and others was at work there. I do not know what or how the Commission reported to Moscow, but from the very fact of its hasty arrival at the Western Front at such a tense time, and from conversation with the members of the Commission, it was not difficult to guess that the Supreme Commander was exceedingly worried about the serious and very dangerous situation which had come to pass in front of Moscow.

Indeed, in the first ten days of

October the forces of our Western, Reserve and Bryansk Fronts had failed badly. It became clear that the Front Commanders had made some serious mistakes: the troops of the Western and Reserve Fronts had stood on the defensive for about six weeks, and had had adequate time to prepare their defences in every respect before the German offensive began, but they had not taken the necessary steps. Their Intelligence had failed to establish correctly the strength and direction of the blows which the enemy was preparing, even though STAVKA had warned them that large groups of German forces were concentrating against them. As a result, even though the enemy offensive had not taken the forces of the Western axis by surprise, nevertheless the largest possible forces for defence in depth had not been concentrated in good time on the threatened axes.

Artillery interlude: German gunners bombard Kaluga

Above all the backbone of a defensive system, anti-tank defence, had not been built up, nor had Front Reserves been brought up to those places; no artillery or air counter-preparation had been organised to smash the forces of the main enemy group while they were still in their starting areas; and when our defence was broken in the Vyazma area, the Command did not withdraw the forces which were threatened with encirclement. As a result Sixteenth, Twentieth, Twenty-fourth and Thirty-second Armies had been surrounded.

While I was talking to the members of the Commission, I was handed an order to telephone the Supreme Commander, and went out into the conference room. Now Stalin himself mentioned his decision to appoint me Commander of the Western Front, and asked me whether I had any objections. I had no reason to object. However, it became clear as the conversation went on that Stalin intended to change the leadership

completely, and remove the previous Command of the Front. I did not think this was the best solution in the circumstances, and made the suggestions, to which Stalin agreed, that I S Konev should remain as Deputy Commander, and also that it would be very useful to send him as Deputy Commander of the Western Front to take charge of the group of forces on the Kalinin axis, which was too far away from the headquarters and needed an additional control. I was told that the remaining forces of Reserve Front, the units deployed in the Mozhaysk line, and the STAVKA Reserves which were on their way towards it, were being handed over to Western Front.

'Form the Western Front as quickly as possible, and get to work,' was how Stalin ended the conversation.

When I had discussed the situation with Konev and Sokolovsky, we decided to withdraw the Front headquarters to Alabino; to send Konev with the necessary means of control and a group of officers to co-ordinate operations on the Kalinin axis; and that I and the Member of Military Council, Bulganin, would go to Mozhaysk to the Commander of the Mozhaysk Fortified Zone, Colonel S I Bogdanov, so as to familiarise ourselves with the situation on the spot.

The headquarters of the Mozhaysk Fortified Zone, where we arrived during the afternoon of 10th October, was located in the town House of Culture, from which the artillery cannonade and the explosion of bombs could be heard clearly. Colonel Bogdanov reported that the 32nd Rifle Division, reinforced by artillery and a tank brigade, was in action with German mechanised and armoured forward units on the approaches to Borodino. It was commanded by Colonel VI Polosukhin, a very experienced officer. After ordering Bogdanov to hold on at any price we returned to the Front headquarters in Alabino.

Here large-scale organisational and operational work was already under way, aiming to establish a stable defence along the line Volokolamsk-Mozhaysk-Maloyaroslavets-Kaluga as a matter of urgency, to develop it in depth, and to create some reserves.

From the operational and tactical point of view the Mozhaysk defence line had a number of undoubted advantages. In front of its forward edge flowed the Rivers Lama, Moskva, Kolocha, Luzha and Sukhodrev. Since their banks were cut back vertically, all these rivers were serious obstacles to tanks. To the rear of the Mozhaysk line was a well-developed system of roads and railways, which facilitated broad manoeuvring by forces on all axes. Here it was possible to create a multi-zoned defence, in which resistance to the enemy would increase as he penetrated into its depths.

But the trouble was that the Mozhaysk line, which was 135 miles long, had very few troops in it by 10th October. The forces deployed by that time amounted altogether to only four rifle divisions, the Moscow Artillery and Military-Political Schools, the School named after the Supreme Soviet of the RSFSR, the Podolsk Machine Gun School, three reserve rifle regiments and five machine gun battalions. In sum, the line was occupied by forty-five battalions instead of the 150 for which it was designed, making for a negligible density of forces, on average one battalion to three miles of front. Thus the approach to Moscow was in fact not covered.

However, STAVKA took extraordinary measures to meet the threat hanging over the capital. On 9th October the Command of Forces of the Mozhaysk Defence Line, was renamed Command of the Moscow Reserve Front (Front Commander, Lieutenant-General PA Artemyev, Member of Military Council, Divisional Commissar KF Telegin, Chief of Staff, Major-General AI Kudryashov) STAVKA directed thither five newly-formed machine gun battalions, ten anti-tank artillery regiments and five tank brigades. By 11th October the forces on the Mozhaysk Line had been joined into the Fifth Army under the Command of Major-General DD Lelyushenko. Retreating formations of the Western and Reserve Fronts were concentrated on this defensive line, while units and formations from the right wing of the Western Front and from the southwestern direction, as well as reserves from the depths of the country, were hastily re-deployed to it. At the call of the Party and Government the entire country, the sons and daughters of all the Union Republics, rose to defend Moscow.

The command of the Western Front now had to cope properly with the forces and weapons which were coming to it, without losing a minute of valuable time, to prepare a stable defence on all threatened axes, develop it in depth, and accumulate front reserves which would permit manoeuvre for strengthening vulner-

able points in the defence.

All of us had to work day and night without pause. Men were literally collapsing from tiredness and lack of sleep, but all did everything possible, and sometimes even the impossible. Moved by the feeling that we were personally responsible for the fate of Moscow, and the fate of the Mother-land, the generals and staff officers, commanders and political workers of all ranks, showed unprecedented energy and self-sacrifice. They tried to ensure that everything was done in the best way possible, that air and ground reconnaissance were carried out, that the troops of the front were given firm leadership, that the flow of supplies was uninterrupted, Party political work was developed, the morale of the men was raised, every soldier had implanted in his mind confidence in the forces to which he belonged and certainty that the enemy would be defeated on the approaches to Moscow.

Left and above: Old and young, in all weathers, the Muscovites grimly prepare their defences. Often fires have to be lit to thaw the ground sufficiently as the temperature drops ever lower

In accordance with a STAVKA directive all combat units and installations of Moscow Reserve Front were handed over to the reconstituted Western Front with effect from 2300 hours on 12th October. In the meantime the situation was becoming more and more difficult. Here is one of the reports made by the Military Council of the Front on 12th October 1941 to the STAVKA, which shows how things were: 'The enemy, in a strength of two Panzer and one motorised infantry divisions with not less than three infantry divisions, has captured the Sychevka-Zubtsov area, and is continuing to develop his success towards Kalinin. The forward units of one Panzer division moving towards Kalinin reached a line twenty-five kilometres southeast of Staritsa at 9.35 on 12th October.

Decisions taken and orders given: 1. The Commanders of Twenty-second and Twenty-ninth Armies are each to send forward in vehicles one regiment with anti-tank weapons to the area east of Staritsa to cover the Kalinin axis. 2. 174th Rifle Division, which was on its way to the town of Rzhev, has been sent to Staritsa. 3. The Commander of Twenty-second Army has been ordered to withdraw 256th Rifle Division from the front and send it to Kalinin by forced march to defend Kalinin from the south. 4. The Commander of the Kalinin Garrison has been ordered to deploy detachments from the Garrison on the line Boriskovo-Pokrovskoye . . .

The Defence of Kalinin may be strengthened only by the immediate despatch to Kalinin of not less than one rifle division and a tank brigade. The Front cannot at present do this.

I request you to order the rapid despatch of a division to Kalinin from the Supreme Command Reserve.

The Volokolamsk axis, where there are absolutely no troops, is in the same position, and the Front can spare nothing for this axis.

It is essential to provide not less than one division immediately for this axis also.'

In mid-October the reconstituted Fifth, Sixteenth, Forty-third and Forty-ninth Armies amounted altogether to only 90,000 men. These forces were far from adequate for a continuous defence, and so we decided that in the first instance we would cover the main axes: Volokolamsk, Istra, Mozhaysk, Maloyaroslavets, and Podolsk-Kaluga. The bulk of artillery and anti-tank weapons were concentrated on the same axes.

On 13th October Headquarters Sixteenth Army headed by KK Rokossovsky, AA Lobachev and MS Malinin was set up on the Voloko-

lamsk axis. The Volokolamsk Fortified Zone and newly arriving units were incorporated into Sixteenth Army. In Fifth Army, under the command of Major-General L A Govorov, were included the Mozhaysk Fortified Zone, Colonel Polosukhin's 32nd Rifle Division and newly arriving units, while Forty-third Army was headed by Major-General K D Golubev, and the Maloyaroslavets Fortified Zone was included in it. Forty-ninth Army was commanded by Lieutenant-General IG Zakharkin, and incorporated the Kaluga Fortified Zone.

These commanders were all experienced leaders, knew their business, and could be absolutely relied on to do everything possible with the troops entrusted to them to prevent an

A cavalry unit clatters through Moscow on its way to the front

enemy breakthrough to Moscow. I must also mention the precise work of the Headquarters staff headed by Lieutenant-General Sokolovsky, now Marshal of the Soviet Union, and the energetic efforts made by the Chief of Signals Troops of the Front, Major-General ND Psurtsev (now the Minister of Communications) to ensure that control of the Front's forces was solidly based.

Behind the Western Front's first echelon a great deal of engineering work was going on to develop defence in depth, and anti-tank zones were being set up on all axes that were vulnerable to tanks, while reserves were being brought up on to the main axes. The front headquarters moved from Alabino to Perkhushkovo, from

where telephone and telegraph lines extended to the ground and air forces. Supplies were hastily brought up, and medical and other rear installations were being developed. Thus a new Western Front was created, and its mission was to fend off the German attack on Moscow.

The Communist Party did a great deal of work in explaining to the Soviet people the seriousness of the situation, and the imminence of the threat hanging over Moscow. The Central Committee called on the whole people to wage a decisive struggle against indifference and panic, to carry out their duty to the Motherland honourably, and not to let the enemy through to Moscow.

In the middle of October our most

important need was time to prepare our defences. Looking at the actions of Nineteenth, Sixteenth, Twentieth, Twenty-fourth, Thirty-second Armies and Boldin's group, which were surrounded west of Vyazma, then one must give their heroic fight its due. Although they were in the enemy rear they did not lay down their weapons, but continued to fight bravely and attempted to break through to join up with units of the Red Army, thus tying up large enemy forces and preventing the Germans from developing their offensive towards Moscow. The Front Command and STAVKA assisted the encircled troops in their fight by bombarding German positions from the air, and dropping food and ammunition from aircraft, but neither the Front nor STAVKA could do any more for the encircled troops at that time, since they had neither forces nor weapons to spare.

Twice – on 10th and 12th October – we broadcast cypher telegrams to the Army Commanders of the encircled forces, giving brief reports on the enemy and setting them the task of breaking out under the overall control of General Lukin, the Commander of Nineteenth Army. He was told to report in cypher at once his plan and force grouping for a breakout, and to tell us on which sector we were to arrange for support by the Front air force. However, neither of our messages was answered. They probably arrived too late; it seems that the encircled armies were no longer under control, and the troops succeeded in breaking out of encirclement only in isolated groups.

Nevertheless, thanks to the stubbornness and steadfastness shown by our troops fighting in encirclement in the Vyazma area, the enemy's main forces were held up during the days that were most critical for us. We gained valuable time for organising defence on the Mozhaysk line, and thus the blood of the troops in the encircled force was not shed in vain, but the achievement of the Soviet soldiers whose heroic fight at Vyazma contributed so greatly to the general cause of defending Moscow, still awaits its chronicler.

On 13th October our units gave up Kaluga under the German onslaught. On all the main axes fierce fighting blazed up, as the Germans hurled a large part of their mobile forces onto all routes leading to Moscow. Front intelligence reported that on 15th October, up to fifty tanks reached the Turginovo area, about one hundred, Lotoshino, up to one hundred, Makarovo and Karagatovo, about fifty Borovsk, and about forty Borodino.

Because of the increased danger to the capital, the Central Committee of the Party and the State Defence Committee decided to evacuate at once several departments of the Central Committee and the government, as well as the whole of the diplomatic corps, from Moscow to Kuybyshev; and also to remove the most important state treasures. The evacuation began on the night of 15th–16th October. The Muscovites reacted to all these measures with full understanding, but every flock has its black sheep, and so there were cowards, panic-mongers and self-seekers to be found. These fled out of Moscow in every direction spreading panicky rumours that it was about to fall, and so, to mobilise the forces and people of the capital to repel the enemy, and also to put an end to the panic which *provocateurs* had caused on 16th October in Moscow, the State Defence Committee on 19th October proclaimed Moscow and adjacent areas to be in a state of siege.

The Volokolamsk-Mozhaysk-Maloyaroslavets-Serpukhov Defence Line was occupied by forces which were still very weak, and in places the enemy had already seized it. To prevent his breaking through to Moscow, the Military Council of the Front selected as the main defensive

Men and guns: the new reserves of the Red Army parade in Moscow

position the line from Novo-Zavidovsky, through Klin, the Istra reservoir, Istra, Zhavoronki, Krasnaya Pakhra, and Serpukhov to Alexin. In view of the importance of this decision I think I should give here in full the plan for withdrawing Western Front's armies from the Mozhaysk defence line. It was approved by Stalin on 19th October and envisaged:

1. If it proves impossible to hold the enemy's offensive on the Mozhaysk defence line the Armies of the Front, resisting the attacking enemy with rearguards, are to withdraw their main forces, beginning with the main mass of artillery, to the defence line which is being prepared along the line Novo-Zavidovsky-Klin the Istra reservoir-Istra-Zhavoronki-Krasnaya Pakhra-Serpukhov-Alexin. All air strength is to be used to cover the withdrawal.

2. Until their units are deployed on the main defence line, the armies are to organise and fight battles with strong rearguards, well supplied with anti-tank weapons, and with mobile units for counterattacking at short notice held available in each army, are to delay the enemy for as long as possible on the intermediate line Kozlovo-Gologuzovo-Yelgozino-Novo-Petrov-skoye-Kolubyakovo-Naro-Fominsk-Tarutino-Chernaya Gryaz-Protva river.

3. The armies are to withdraw within their own lines of demarcation, except for Sixteenth and Fifth: the line of demarcation between these is established as Zagorsk, Iksha. Povarovo, Tarkhanovo, all inclusive to Sixteenth Army.

4. The rear services of the armies will withdraw to the east within their boundaries, except for Fifth and Thirty-third Armies, whose rear services follow roads which must be outside Moscow and the Moscow complex, that is the rear services of Fifth Army – along the roads north of Khimki and Mytishchi, and of Thirty-third Army south of Peredelkino and Lyubertsy. Not a single cart or vehicle

is to be directed or admitted through Moscow or the Moscow complex. To ensure this Fifth and Thirty-third Armies will establish firm and timely regulation for the withdrawal, and lay down the routes along which transport, rear organisations and troops are to move. Unnecessary rear organisations are to be withdrawn in advance of time.

5. If the battle on the main line Istra-Pavlovskaya - Sloboda - Zhavoronki turns out unfavourably, Fifth Army must retreat not to the fortified perimeter around Moscow, but to the northeast north of Khimki, and

The Red Army's greatest asset: a snow-camouflaged T-34 tank

its left flank on to units of Thirty-third Army south of Peredelkino and Lyubertsy. Those units are to be withdrawn to army reserve, passing around the Moscow Fortified Zone from southeast and east to the Pushkino area.

6. Consequent on this the supply base of Fifth Army must be Pushkino Station and that of Thirty-third Ramenskoye Station. Sixteenth, Forty-third and Forty-ninth Armies must base themselves on supply stations within their demarcation lines.

7. To cover the planned withdrawal of units of the Armies along the network of roads Novo Petrovskoye-Kubinka-Naro-Fominsk-Vorobya, anti-tank defence by artillery regiments of the anti-tank defence forces must be arranged in advance. This must exclude any possibility of an enemy Panzer breakthrough into the rear.

Part of the Armies' forces will occupy the main defence line on the most important axes in advance, both with infantry units, and especially with artillery and rocket batteries.

Sixteenth Army will deploy the remnants of 126th Rifle Division in line in the Klin and Troitskoye areas in advance; Fifth Army will do the same in the Davidkovo and Krasnaya Pakhra areas with 110th or 113th Rifle Division; and Forty-third Army in the area west of Podolsk and Lopasnya with 53rd Rifle Division. 8. Control of the Armies by the Front during the withdrawal will be arranged via the communications net of the People's Commissariat of Defence in Moscow; simultaneously a communications net and location for front headquarters are to be prepared in the area Orekhovo-Zuyevo or Likino-Dulevo. (Signed) Commander of Western Front, Army General Zhukov, Member of Military Council of Western Front, Bulganin, Chief of Staff Western Front, Lieutenant-General Sokolovsky, 19th October 1941.

This plan was conveyed to the army commanders under conditions of particular secrecy, and they worked out their own plans in accordance with it. However, as we know, although STAVKA confirmed it, the withdrawal from the Mozhaysk line had to be carried out by the Front's forces in very hard fighting, in which they attempted to delay the enemy for as long as possible, and gain maximum time to concentrate the formations which were coming up from STAVKA reserve and to reinforce the rear defence line.

The Military Council of Western Front then issued an exhortation to its troops, in which it said: 'Comrades! in the threatening hour of danger for our state, the life of every soldier belongs to the Motherland. The Motherland demands from each of us the greatest intensity of strength, bravery, heroism and steadfastness. The Motherland calls on us to become an indestructible wall and block the road of the Fascist hordes to our

A Russian tank unit takes over its new KV heavy tanks from the collective farmers whose savings paid for them

beloved Moscow. Now as never before vigilance, iron discipline, organisation, decisiveness of action, unshakable will to victory and readiness for self-sacrifice are demanded.

I do not think there is any need for me to describe the course of the battle, since it has been described many times in detail in a number of historical works and in books. Well known, too, is the outcome of the October defensive battles in front of Moscow. In a month of fierce and bloody fighting the German forces succeeded in advancing in general about 230–250 kilometres. However, the Nazi Command's plan to capture Moscow was disrupted, the enemy forces were seriously worn out, and their assault groups were overstretched. The German offensive lost more and more of its impetus every

Food for the guns: women workers check the calibre of freshly-machined shells

day, and by the end of October it was stopped along a front line running from Turginovo through Volokolamsk, Dorokhovo, Naro-Fominsk, west of Serpukhov to Alexin. In the Kalinin area the Kalinin Front's forces had also stabilised the defence by that time. (Because of the great extent of the Western Front and the difficulties which arose in controlling the forces in the Kalinin area, STAVKA decided on 17th October to group together the Twenty-second, Twenty-ninth and Thirtieth Armies under the command of a new Kalinin Front, commanded by Colonel-General Konev, with Corps-Commissar D S Leonov as Member of Military Council and Major-General I I Ivanov as Chief of Staff).

Bryansk Front, whose forces had retreated by 30th October to the line Alexin-Tula-Efremov-Tim, disrupted the enemy's plan to seize Tula and covered the routes towards Yelets and Voronezh.

When we speak of heroic achieve-

ments, we do not mean only those of our splendid soldiers, officers and political workers. What was achieved in the front in October, and then in the battles which followed, became possible thanks to the unity and common efforts of the Soviet troops, the workers of the capital and of Moscow Region, unanimously supported by the whole people of the entire country.

The diverse activities of the party organisation of Moscow and its Region, uniting and raising the masses of workers to defend the capital against a cruel enemy, merged together into a heroic epic. The inspiring slogans of the Central Committee of the Party, the Moscow city and Oblast Party Organisations, were near to every Muscovite, every soldier and all Soviet people, and found a profound response in their hearts. The workers of Moscow, together with the soldiers, took an oath to stand to the death, and prevent the enemy reaching the capital, and this oath they fulfilled with honour.

Let us remember that in October–November 1941 alone the workers of the capital provided the front with five divisions of reinforcements. Altogether since the beginning of the war the Muscovites had formed seventeen divisions. Apart from volunteer divisions of the People's Militia, they created and armed hundreds of detachments, of combat groups, and tank destroyer detachments, against the possibility of an enemy breakthrough to the city. On 13th October 1941 the Party Aktiv of the capital resolved to create workers' battalions in each urban region. And soon, literally within a few days, twenty-five independent companies and battalions had come into existence, with about 12,000 fighters in their ranks, the bulk of them Communists and Communist Youth League members. Yet another 100,000 Moscow workers went through military training in their spare time and were then drafted to combat units, while about 17,000 women and

girls trained as nurses and members of medical teams.

There were specialists in diverse peaceful trades, among them cadre workers, engineers, technicians and scholars or workers in art – naturally far from all of them were used to military ways. Military service was a novelty for them, and they were already in action while they still had much to learn. But they had something in common, something in which they all stood out, a high patriotism, an unshakable steadfastness and a belief in victory. And was it a coincidence, that from the volunteer combat units formed in the capital, the splendid formation of Muscovite volunteers was created after they had gained combat experience? Muscovites made up the nucleus of many specialised sub-units of intelligence, were skiers, and worked with partisan detachments.

The achievements of the capital's inhabitants, who with their own hands built defence installations to protect it, can never be forgotten. More than 500,000 workers of Moscow and Moscow Region, the majority of them women, built defences on the distant and close approaches to the city.

In the years since the war Nazi generals and bourgeois historians have had a great deal to say about Russian bad roads and mud on the one hand, and the Russian frost on the other. This kind of myth-making has already been properly discredited, nevertheless I would like yet again to draw the attention of readers to what General Tippelskirch has written, claiming it as the element which prevented the Nazi forces from capturing Moscow: 'To move along the roads became impossible,' he writes 'the mud stuck to our feet, to the hooves of the animals, to the wheels of carts and vehicles . . . the offensive came to a halt.'

When the Nazi generals were planning their expedition to the east, did they really expect to ride the

Bound for the front: riflemen and anti-tank gunners march out of Moscow

whole way to Moscow and beyond on smooth and well-surfaced roads? Well, if they did, so much the worse for them and for the Nazi forces which, as Tippelskirch claims, were brought to a halt by the mud on the approaches to Moscow. In those days I saw with my own eyes thousands and thousands of women citizens of Moscow, most of whom were not accustomed to heavy civil engineering, and who had come lightly clothed from their apartments in the city. In that same bad weather and mud they were digging anti-tank ditches and trenches, erecting anti-tank obstacles, putting up barricades and entanglements, and dragging sandbags. The mud stuck to their feet too, and to the wheels of the barrows in which they transported the earth, and made the shovels, which were not made for women's hands anyway, incomparably heavier . . . I don't think I need push the comparison any further, but I may add, for the benefit of those who want to hide the real reasons for their defeat under the mud, that in October 1941 the season of bad roads was relatively short. The cold weather began early in November, snow fell, and terrain and roads became passable everywhere. In the November days of the German 'general offensive' the temperature in the Moscow combat area levelled out at seven to ten degrees of frost, and

everybody knows that at those temperatures there isn't any mud.

But the Muscovites kept on working self-sacrificingly even in the frost, erecting defence installations. Construction of the outer perimeter in the Moscow defence zone was completed by 25th November. And here, as I knew, over 100,000 Muscovites, predominantly women, worked. In that line they built 1,428 artillery and machine-gun emplacements and nests, 160 kilometres of anti-tank ditches, 112 kilometres of three-row barbed wire entanglements, and a large number of other obstacles. However, this was not all they contributed to our common victory. The readiness of the workers to sacrifice themselves in defence of their capital had a great

moral effect on the troops, multiplying their strength and reinforcing their will to fight.

Every day we heard of the self-sacrificing labour of the Muscovites, who in almost all Moscow's factories set up equipment for manufacturing and war production was undertaken not only in large factories but in those of the local industry and industrial co-operatives.

Nor can I forget to mention that thousands of Muscovites in the Civil Defence detachments and teams spent day and night on watch on the roofs. Hundreds of women and girls worked voluntarily in hospitals, restoring wounded soldiers to health and surrounding them with care and devotion. And what pleasure was evoked at the front by the letters, telegrams and parcels from Muscovites and from the workers of our entire country! During the battle for Moscow the troops received 450,000 parcels, and 700,000 articles of clothing, including some from workers of the Mongolian People's Republic, a delegation from which, headed by Marshal Choibalsan, arrived at our Front.

On 1st November I was summoned to STAVKA. Stalin said: 'Apart from the ceremonial gathering on the anniversary of the October Revolution, we want to hold a military parade in Moscow as well. What do you think? Will the situation at the Front allow us to have these celebrations?'

I reported that during the coming days the enemy would be in no position to start a large offensive, since he had suffered heavy casualties during the October battle and was now busy reinforcing and regrouping his forces. As for his Air Force, it could be active during those days and very likely would try to be.

It was therefore decided to strengthen the capital's air defences by bringing in additional fighters from neighbouring Fronts, and the traditional parade of troops was held on Red Square. Everything went off well and after the ceremonial march past the Lenin mausoleum the units and formations went to the Front. Both the internal and international significance of this October parade were undoubtedly immense.

In the first half of November the Soviet Supreme Command, which expected the enemy to try again to attack Moscow, continued to take all steps possible in the circumstances to ensure that he failed. The forces of the Western Front continued to strengthen the defence lines which they occupied, and there were some regroupings. From 1800 hours on 10th November Fiftieth Army and the defence of Tula were handed over to Western Front by decision of the STAVKA, and Bryansk Front was dissolved (its Third and Thirteenth Armies were incorporated in Southwestern Front). The transfer to us of the Tula sector together with Fiftieth Army meant that our defensive front was considerably extended, especially as this army was numerically very weak. However, new formations, equipment, arms, ammunition, communications materials and supplies continued to come to us from STAVKA Reserve. Fur coats, felt boots, warm underwear, warm jackets, and fur hats with ear flaps arrived in great quantities at the Front, army and forward stores. In mid-November our troops were warmly clad and felt somewhat more comfortable than the soldiers of Nazi Germany, who were muffled up in warm clothing requisitioned from the civilian population. In those days vast straw 'galoshes' began to appear on many of the German soldiers, and these made their movements very slow. Nonetheless, all our information indicated that the Germans had nearly finished regrouping, and we had to expect that they would soon resume their offensive.

The additional rifle and armoured formations which we had received from STAVKA Reserve were concentrated on the most dangerous axes, above all Volokolamsk-Klin and Istra, where we expected the main armoured

attack to come. The 17th, 18th, 20th, 24th and 44th Cavalry Divisions arrived for Sixteenth Army, and were deployed on the Volokolamsk-Klin axis, while additional forces were also brought up to the Tula-Serpukhov area, where we expected Second Panzer and Fourth Armies to strike. On 9th November the Cavalry Corps of General P A Belov, 415th Rifle and 112th Tank Divisions and 33rd Tank Brigade arrived on the left wing of the front. I must point out here that although the Western Front had been reinforced on a large scale and had six armies by the middle of November, its defence had little depth to it, especially in the centre, since our front line was more than 375 miles long. So we tried in the first instance to use these forces for protecting the most threatened axes on the flanks, and where possible to allocate something to Front Reserve, so that we could manoeuvre if necessary. However, the Supreme Commander's order which came through on 13th November, forced us to make some radical alterations to our plans. Stalin telephoned: 'How's the enemy behaving?' he asked me.

'He's nearly finished preparing his assault groups, and it looks as if he will start the offensive soon,' I replied.

'And where are you expecting the main attack?'

'We expect the most powerful attack from the Volokolamsk-Novo-Petrovskoye area, making for Klin ahd Istra. Guderian's army will probably strike to outflank Tula and make for Venev and Kashira.'

'Shaposhnikov (The Chief of General Staff) and I think,' said Stalin 'that we must disrupt the assault which the enemy is preparing by our own pre-emptive counterstrike. One counterattack must go to outflank Volokolamsk from the north, and the other from the Serpukhov area into the flank of German Fourth Army. It is clear that big forces are assembling in those areas to strike for Moscow.'

'From where are the forces for these

counterattacks to come?' I asked. 'The Front has no troops to spare. The forces we have are only enough to hold the positions we occupy now.'

'In the Volokolamsk area use the right flank formations of Rokossovsky's army, the 58th Tank Division, the Independent Cavalry Divisions and Dovator's Cavalry Corps. In the Serpukhov area use Belov's Cavalry Corps, Getman's Tank Division and part of Forty-ninth Army,' suggested Stalin.

'We can't do that just now,' I replied, 'we can't throw the Front's last reserves into dubious counterattacks. We will have nothing left for reinforcing our armies when the enemy's assault groups attack.'

'You have six armies in your Front. Isn't that enough?'

I replied that the defensive front of the Western Front's troops was very extended, and including its indentations was at present more than 375 miles, while we had very few reserves

New masses of infantry on the march beside the Moscow river

in depth, especially in the centre of the front.

'Consider the question of counterattacks settled. Let me have your plan this evening' – and that was Stalin's final word on the matter.

I tried again to convince Stalin of the senselessness of counterattacking with our last reserves, arguing that the terrain north of Volokolamsk was unsuitable. But he rang off.

This conversation left me depressed, not, of course, because the Supremo had disagreed with my opinion, but because Moscow, which the troops had sworn to defend to their last drop of blood, was in mortal danger, while we had been categorically ordered to throw our last reserves into very dubious counterattacks. If we expended them, we would not be able to strengthen weak points in the defence.

Within fifteen minutes the Member

of Military Council, Bulganin, came to me. It seemed that the Supreme Commander had rung him up immediately after the conversation with me, and had said: 'You and Zhukov there are getting too big for your boots. But we'll put you in your places.' Stalin ordered him to get together with me at once to arrange the counterattacks.

Within two hours the Front headquarters had issued the order to the commanders of Sixteenth and Forty-ninth Armies and the other formations for the counterattacks, and reported accordingly to STAVKA. The counterattacks were mounted, but literally on their heels on 15th November, the Nazi command renewed the offensive against Moscow. The course of the battle in those days will be well known to readers, and therefore I shall recount only some details and episodes which fill out the general picture.

As is well known, the enemy assault northwest of Moscow struck at the left flank of Kalinin Front's Thirtieth Army, which had very weak defences south of the 'Moscow Sea', and simultaneously at the right flank and centre of the Sixteenth Army of the Western Front. More than 300 tanks were operating against these armies, while they had only fifty-six, and those were light and weakly armed.

The Germans broke through Thirtieth Army and began to develop their offensive at high speed in the general direction of Klin from the morning of 16th November. We had no reserves here. On the same day a powerful enemy blow from the Volokolamsk area on the Istra axis followed. Here the enemy threw in 400 medium and heavy tanks, while our forces had about 150 medium and light tanks.

On 17th November at 2300 STAVKA transferred the Thirtieth Army from Kalinin to Western Front, thus extending the defences of the latter even further northwards, right up to the Moscow Sea. By the evening of 23rd November the enemy had taken Klin after a fierce battle and was heading towards Dmitrov, while some of the tanks had turned towards Solnechnogorsk. On 25th November Sixteenth Army withdrew from Solnechnogorsk. To that area, to the disposal of General Rokossovsky, the Military Council of the Front redeployed everything that it could from other sectors, including individual platoons and groups of soldiers and anti-tank rifles, individual groups of tanks, artillery batteries, and anti-aircraft batteries withdrawn from the Moscow area. The situation became critical. Our defensive front was bending inwards, we were becoming very weak in some places, so it seemed that the irrevocable was taking place. But no! The Soviet troops fought with tremendous bravery and held out until the 7th Division arrived in the Solnechnogorsk area from Serpukhov, with two tank brigades and two anti-tank artillery regiments from STAVKA Reserve. After receiving these reinforcements our troops again established an impassable defensive front. In the first days of December it seemed from the character of the fighting and the strength of the German blows that the enemy was becoming exhausted, and no longer had either troops or resources for serious offensive operations on this axis.

Events on the other axes developed in an almost equally intense way, for here the enemy forces struck their main blows. The divisions of the right wing of the German Volokolamsk group reached the area five miles northeast of Zvenigorod on 2nd December, but on the following day were no longer capable of advancing. To co-operate with the attacking forces the enemy on 1st December went over to the offensive on the previously passive sector near Naro-Fominsk. He succeeded in breaking through the front of Thirty-third

New hitting-power: a heavy Russian gun mounted on a tracked carriage

The *Wehrmacht* struggles in its not-so-private hell of snow and slush. *Right:* The Russians also felt the cold: a Soviet tank crew in a lull in the fighting

Army and reaching the area of Apre-levka, but on 3rd–4th December counterattacks by units of Fifth, Thirty-third and Forty-third Armies defeated the enemy forces which had broken through and threw them back to the western bank of the Nara river.

On the Maloyaroslavets and Serpukhov axes our troops went on fighting fiercely to repel the enemy offensive between 16th November and 2nd December. Up to 30th November heavy fighting was going on in the areas of Kashira and Mordves, after which the Commander of Second Panzer Army, General Guderian, ordered it on to the defensive. The Soviet forces repelled all enemy assaults in the Tula area, did him severe damage and prevented him from breaking through towards Moscow.

The Germans ignored their losses but dashed on headlong, in an attempt to break through to Moscow with their Panzer wedges at any price. But thanks to good co-operation between formations and units of all arms of service our deeply echelonned artillery and anti-tank defence withstood this fierce onslaught. Many thousands of German corpses were scattered over the battlefields, but nowhere did their troops succeed in breaking through to Moscow. In the process of battle Soviet forces were withdrawn in due order to lines which had been prepared in advance and occupied by the artillery, and again fought stubbornly for them, repelling furious attacks.

In Moscow the State Defence Committee, part of the leadership of the Party Central Committee, and the Council of People's Commissars, continued to function. The workers laboured stubbornly for twelve-eighteen hours a day, supplying the

Fronts which were defending the capital with weapons, equipment, ammunition and other material resources, repairing equipment and tanks.

I don't remember the date exactly, but it was very shortly after the largest German tactical breakthrough, in the sector of Thirtieth Army and on the right flank of Rokossovsky's army, so I think it was 19th November, Stalin rang me up and asked: 'Are you sure that we can hold Moscow? It grieves me to have to ask you this. Speak frankly, as a Communist.'

'Of course we shall hold Moscow. But we need not less than two more armies and at least 200 tanks.'

'I'm glad you are so confident,' concluded Stalin. 'Ring Shaposhnikov and agree with him where to concentrate the two reserve armies which you asked for. They will be ready by the end of November, but for the moment we haven't any tanks.'

Within half an hour Shaposhnikov and I had agreed that the First Shock Army which was then being formed would be concentrated in the Yakhroma area, and the Tenth in the Ryazan region.

By 5th December German forces on all the Western Front's sectors had become exhausted, and they began to take up the defensive under our attacks. In essence this signified the failure of Hitler's plans for a lightning war. Inability to complete all the strategic operations on the Soviet-German front lowered morale in the German forces, and aroused their first doubts about the possibility of winning the war. The Nazi leadership was discredited in the eyes of world public opinion. The Soviet forces, inspired by their successes in the defensive battles and their success in protecting Moscow began the counteroffensive without a pause of any kind. This was a great and joyful event, which stirred not only the Soviet people and

its soldiers, but many other people throughout the world. But before I talk about that, I would like to touch on another question.

It is said in some works of military history that the battles fought by the Western, Reserve and Bryansk Fronts in October should not be included in the Battle of Moscow. It is also claimed that the Germans had been completely stopped on the Mozhaysk defence line by the end of October or the beginning of November, and that the Nazi High Command had to prepare a new 'general offensive operation' for the attack on Moscow. I cannot agree at all with statements of this kind.

In undertaking the October operation on the Moscow axis, codenamed 'Typhoon', the German High Command counted on defeating the Soviet forces on the Vyazma-Moscow and Bryansk-Moscow axes, and seizing Moscow in the shortest possible time by outflanking it from north and

south. As to the form and method of the operation they intended to achieve this strategic aim in sequence by means of double envelopment. The first encirclement and defeat of Soviet forces was to take place in the Bryansk-Vyazma area; the second encirclement and the capture of Moscow was to be achieved by the emergence of panzer groups from the northwest through Klin and from the south through Tula and Kashira, thus closing the pincers of strategic encirclement in the Noginsk area.

At the beginning of October the Germans completely achieved their immediate aim, in the basis of their superiority in manpower and equipment and by exploiting the mistakes made by the Fronts. As for their final strategic aim – the capture of Moscow – it was not achieved because the main forces were delayed by the need to fight the Soviet troops encircled in the Vyazma area (units of Nineteenth, Sixteenth, Twentieth, Twenty-fourth,

Thirty-second Armies and Boldin's group.) The limited forces which the enemy threw in to break the Mozhaysk line and emerge in the Moscow area succeeded only in pushing back the Soviet forces to the line Volokolamsk-Dorokhovo-Protva river-the River Nara-Alexin-Tula, but they did not fulfil their task of breaking through.

The argument that during November the Germans had to replenish their forces and supplies on a large scale and to regroup some of the panzer formations on their left wing, can to my mind in no way serve as an adequate basis for concluding that they had to prepare a 'new general offensive'. For it is well known that such measures are normal in all strategic offensive operations, and therefore cannot be the factors which determine their beginning and their end.

Since the war I have frequently been asked how the Soviet forces succeeded in holding the onslaught by the

Left: **By the first days of December the pace of the** *Wehrmacht* **had been reduced to a crawl.** *Above:* **With the German spearheads in the suburbs, Muscovite Young Communists tighten their city's defences**

strongest German assault groups towards Moscow. A good deal has been written, most of it correct, about the course of the defensive battle in front of Moscow. However, as the former Commander of Western Front, I would like to express my opinion.

The Nazi Supreme Command, in planning a complicated and large-scale strategic operation such as was Typhoon, seriously underestimated the forces, state and capability of the Soviet Army to fight for Moscow, and grossly overestimated the capabilities of their own forces which had been concentrated to break through our defensive front and capture the Soviet capital. They also committed some gross errors in forming the assault

groups for the second stage of operation Typhoon. Their flank assault groups, especially those which operated in the Tula area, were too weak, and did not have enough infantry. To gamble entirely on panzer formations in the given situation, proved in practice to be erroneous, as they became worn out, suffered heavy casualties, and lost their ability to break through.

The German Command failed to arrange in advance for a pinning-down attack in the centre of our front, even though it had adequate forces to do so. This made it possible for us to transfer all reserves, including divisional reserves, from the central sectors to the flanks of the Front, to fight the enemy assault groups. Their heavy losses, their unpreparedness for fighting in winter conditions, and the fierceness of the Soviet opposition had

a sharp effect upon German battle-worthiness.

By 15th November our Intelligence had succeeded in establishing that assault groups were concentrating on the flanks of the defensive front, and in identifying the axes along which the main attacks would be made. So we opposed them in good time with a deeply echelonned defence, supplied relatively well with anti-tank and engineering resources; here too were concentrated all the main tank units. Our men were profoundly aware that they were personally responsible for Moscow's fate, and the fate of their Motherland and were determined to die rather than let the enemy through to the capital.

A great role was played by the famous decree by the State Defence Committee on 19th October, proclaiming a State of Siege in Moscow

and the areas adjacent to it, and also declaring a decisive struggle for stern discipline and maintenance of due order in all the arms of service defending Moscow. At all command and staff levels we were able to improve the control of the forces considerably, and this assisted them in carrying out their combat assignments with precision.

Immense and fruitful work in organising the defensive operations of the troops of the western strategic direction was carried out by the Operational Directorate of the General Staff, and personally by the Deputy Chief of General Staff, Lieutenant-General AM Vasilevsky. His correct evaluation of the situation on the Western axis in the period 2nd–9th October, and his practical proposals, lay at the basis of STAVKA's measures. Day and night the officers of the

Then, on 5th December, the first Russian counterattacks began

General Staff – both senior and junior – worked untiringly, following every step of the enemy forces and making creative suggestions for eliminating the danger points.

The enemy was unable to break through our defensive front. He did not succeed in surrounding even one division or in firing even one artillery round at Moscow. By the beginning of December he had worn himself out, and had no reserves, while Western Front during this time received from the STAVKA two newly formed armies and a number of formations from which a third army (the Twentieth) was formed. This enabled the Soviet Command to organise a counter-offensive. I shall talk about this in the next chapter.

The Soviet counteroffensive

The German thrust to Moscow had been brought to a halt by the end of November. How close run it had been may be seen by any traveller along the Leningrad highway between Moscow and the International Airport at Sheremetyevo, where a monument 'To the Defenders of Moscow', on the south side of the road indicates the high water mark of the German advance – a raid to Khimki by the motor-cyclists of 62nd Panzer Engineer Regiment. The monument stands at the twenty-three kilometre marker, a mere fourteen-and-a-quarter miles from the Kremlin.

But by the time that dashing foray took place, it was clear to the Germans and to Zhukov that 'Typhoon' had blown itself out. Reports from the combat forces to OKH had referred time after time throughout November to the ferocity of the Soviet resistance, those from SS 'Das Reich', for example, describing the fighting of 19th–20th November as the fiercest and bloodiest of the whole campaign in the east. There were no let-ups, and no sign that the opposition was cracking as Moscow drew nearer. Zhukov's men stood, fought hard, and when forced to

Warmly-clad, snow-camouflaged, well-armed. The Russian winter attacks were a far cry from the disasters of the summer

retreat usually did so in good order, often slipping away unobserved during the night, the departure of the rearguard heralded by the explosion and burning not only of bridges but of the villages and farms in which they had sheltered, and in which the Germans hoped to find protection from the appalling cold on the following night. This tenacity in defence was to become a Zhukov trademark at Stalingrad and Kursk, and while it often amounted to a collective death sentence on entire units, there could be no doubt of its effectiveness in eroding German morale.

However, there was far more to the defensive stage of a Zhukov battle than mere Verdun-type attrition of attacker and defender alike. The grim tenacity, enforced often by threats of dire punishment for unauthorised withdrawal, was not an end in itself. It was a means by which enemy reserves would be drawn in and consumed, until the offensive faltered and died for lack of human fodder. Then, when the enemy was about to take up the defensive, but had not yet dug himself in or taken up a prepared position, the Soviet reserves, carefully husbanded while the units actually used in the defensive stage were worn to shadows, would be let loose on the Germans, fresh troops against exhausted ones, full-strength units against remnants, to be driven forward and forward until they in turn could give no more. Willingness to tolerate heavy casualties in pursuit of high stakes was essential in battles of this scale – every battle led by Zhukov, from Moscow to Berlin, saw over a million troops engaged on each side, and in every one the casualties were large. But the casualties were seldom incurred to no purpose, as so many of them had been in the battle of the frontiers, the Bialystok, Minsk, Smolensk, Uman, Kiev and Azov Coast encirclements, or those at Vyazma and Bryansk, in each of which Soviet forces ranging from 100,000 to over 500,000 were trapped and captured, often by ludicrously small German detachments, with very little to show for their sacrifice. Zhukov's combination of ruthlessness with economy ensured that the Wehrmacht, too, would bleed, whereas in the earlier battles only the Red Army had done so. And in that his casualties brought results, he differed from many of his predecessors. In the Moscow battle he was at his most ruthless, partly perhaps for emotional reasons already discussed, but also because of a lack of resources. As he points out, there were no additional tanks to be had for the counteroffensive, so cavalry and ski troops had to be used as spearheads instead, while it was impossible to provide a single additional man or gun to the three armies in the centre of his front, armies which were already making do without tanks. He mentions also the ammunition shortage, which reduced the artillery rate of fire to one or two rounds per gun per day. In the circumstances, it is perhaps remarkable that any offensive could be mounted, but it was, and with considerable success, for even though no major encirclement was achieved, the fields of the Moscow region were littered with abandoned German equipment, many of Bock's divisions losing over three-quarters of their vehicles and artillery.

The counteroffensive was not a set piece like the later one at Stalingrad, but, as Zhukov says, grew out of the counterattacks which had brought Army Group Centre to a halt at the end of November. Even with the reinforcements from the Far East and the new reserve divisions, comprising between them three armies, First Shock, Tenth and Twentieth, plus the nine rifle and two cavalry divisions, eight rifle and six tank brigades,

Not all Germans suffered in their summer kit—but the few ski-equipped units in the *Wehrmacht* were a drop in the bucket during the long agony of the Moscow battle

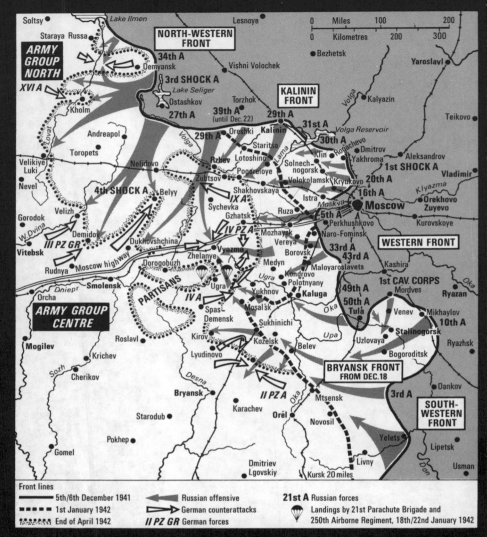

The Battlefronts; December 1941-April 1942

which STAVKA handed over to Zhukov for the counteroffensive, the Red Army possessed no general superiority in manpower. On 1st December Western Front possessed a total combat strength of 577,726 men, Kalinin Front 118,394, while the right wing of Southwestern Front contributed 63,398, for a total of 759,518 combat troops: 1,060,380 including rear services and other non-combatants. A German return of prisoners of war for June–December 1941 shows that in the latter month there were 3,350,639 soldiers of the Red Army in German captivity, more than three times as many as were available in front of Moscow. By contrast, the heading of German troops unaccounted for, which included prisoners as well as missing, totals only 35,875 for the entire period from 22nd June to 31st December 1941, reflecting the failure of the Soviet counteroffensive to achieve a major encirclement. In fact, the frostbite casualties for the winter of 1941–42, at 133,620, were nearly four times as large. Nevertheless, the Wehrmacht had been soundly beaten and driven back from its objective, retreating on some sectors as much as 250 miles between December 1941 and March 1942.

Zhukov's remarks about German attempts to blame the winter weather, rather than the Red Army, for the defeat at Moscow, are as caustic as his earlier comments about the mud. What he says, in effect, is that the German generals should have known about the Russian winter. While there is no doubt that the Wehrmacht was badly handicapped by the lack of winter clothing, as the figures for cases of frostbite confirm, shortage of anti-freeze, suitable lubricants for low temperatures, and even of a suitable' grease for shells and cartridges (that which they used froze, making it necessary to scrape each shell before it would enter the breech, with unfortunate effects upon the rate of fire), it is fair to point out that the handicaps were self-imposed, as

the whole campaign was predicated upon a quick result, and no preparations were made to fight through the winter. From the early days of the 'Marcks plan', it had been expected that the Russians would have been beaten before the *rasputitsa*, in battles mostly fought west of the Dvina-Dnieper line. By the end of the Smolensk battle it should have been clear (the OKH figures presented to Hitler by Halder in July and on 1st December illustrate it unambiguously) that this objective had not been achieved, because the available Soviet reserves had been grossly underestimated by the 'Barbarossa' planners. By then it was probably too late to draw back from the venture, even if the generals had wanted to, and more of them said after the war that they did, than said so at the time. But it was presumably not too late to begin making some preparation for at least clothing the troops for the winter; yet Guderian states that when he indented, in good time, for winter clothing for his men, the indents were not met, and many of his troops were still wearing denims outside Moscow, in fifty to sixty degrees (Fahrenheit) of frost. If the strength of the Red Army was a well-kept secret, the rigours of the Russian winter hardly were, and Zhukov's sarcasm is perhaps understandable. That having been said, it is undeniable that his troops, though no more immune to the cold than the Germans, were more accustomed to it, were properly clad for it, and were provided with equipment that was designed to function in extreme cold. Furthermore numerous German reports attest to systematic destruction by retreating Red Army forces of buildings which might provide shelter for the Germans, showing that the Soviets were aware of the German difficulties and exploited them intelligently - which is, after all, a feature of good generalship.

Zhukov wastes little time on the might-have-beens that have exercised the minds of a number of German

**The Red Air Force hits back:
Sturmovik ground-attack planes
prepare to attack**

generals and Western military historians since the war. He does not, for example, speculate on the possibility that the attack on Moscow might have succeeded, if it had been pursued single-mindedly throughout the summer and autumn campaign. The most he is prepared to say is that 'Typhoon', as conceived and executed, was faulty, in that Guderian's force attacking towards Tula, in an attempt to outflank Moscow from the south, was too weak for its task, especially in infantry, and that the German failure to attack his centre made it possible for him to transfer all his reserves to the flanks, against the Panzer forces. He does not mention the argument advanced by Guderian that if he had not been required to move south to Lokhvitsa, 'Typhoon' could have started early enough to attain most of

its objectives before the '*rasputitsa*'. It is probably wise to follow his example, though perhaps such caution needs a defence. The defence is simply that in dealing with a complicated interaction between opponents, such as a major war, it is not possible to change only one variable. War is more than mathematical problems; the actions of one side are affected by those of the other. Had Army Group Centre pursued a different plan, STAVKA too would have behaved differently. For one thing, to mount 'Typhoon' earlier would have meant forgoing the encirclement of Kirponos's armies at Kiev, would thus have given STAVKA an extra 500,000–600,000 troops, and faced Army Group Centre with a possible flank threat of major dimensions. It would also have necessitated an earlier withdrawal of Panzer Group 4 from the Leningrad Front, thus easing the pressure there before Stalin despatched Zhukov, and leaving Zhukov who, it must be remembered, had just forced the Germans out of the Yelnya salient, in a strong position to attack the flank of any German force attempting to penetrate eastwards past the Reserve Front. As Guderian himself said, in an entirely different context, 'Such trains of thought take a man far from reality'.

Hitler's insistence on standing fast, although opposed by most of the generals at the time, was subsequently accepted by many of them as having been the correct one, which prevented the retreat from becoming a rout. However, having been right on this occasion, Hitler made it a principle, and in the following year, by refusing to allow his beleaguered troops at Stalingrad to withdraw, or even to break out to meet the relieving force which Hoth was leading, doomed the relief expedition to failure and the Sixth and Fourth Panzer Armies to extinction. Thus the expedient which may have preserved much of Army Group Centre from destruction at the hands of Zhukov's forces outside Moscow in 1941, probably helped to make the Marshal's triumph more complete at Stalingrad in 1942. Marshal Zhukov's account of the Soviet counteroffensive and general strategic offensive of winter 1941-42 follows:—

When we talk of the transition by the Soviet forces in front of Moscow from defensive to offensive, we absolutely must remember the specific features of the situation which came into being on the western strategic axis in late November and early December 1941. By that time the German forces which had struck northwest of Moscow and in the Tula area with the task of breaking resistance on the flanks of the Western Front, outflanking Moscow and taking it, were suffering from physical and mental exhaustion, and were on a very extended front. Since they had neither operational nor tactical reserves, the Germans could already no longer count on bringing their offensive to a successful conclusion, even though by inertia they still continued to nibble into our defence. In their rear the partisan movement was becoming more and more active.

However, the situation of the defenders remained extremely tense and strained, for the Soviet forces, which had also suffered large losses, had not yet completely stopped the enemy. They were approaching the very threshold of the capital, and on some sectors the Soviet forward defence line was no more than thirty-one kilometres from it. Consequently the Soviet command could not consider the task of the defensive battle as solved; the enemy had to be stopped once and for all, and stopped whatever happened.

In view of this peculiarity of the situation the counteroffensive by the Soviet forces in front of Moscow was born in the course of the defensive battle itself. It was a continuation of the counterattacks by our troops on the flanks of the front, which began at the end of November and the beginning of December, and the way to conduct it was refined and made more precise as the counterattacks went on.

Until the end of November neither STAVKA nor the Fronts, particularly the Western, whose troops were actually defending Moscow, had worked out a plan for a counteroffensive. During that time all our thoughts and actions were focussed solely on stopping the main enemy forces which had penetrated deeply into our defence, and inflicting such a defeat on them that they would be forced to abandon their offensive.

On 29th November I rang Stalin, and when I had reported the situation, asked him to issue an order subordinating to the Western Front the First Shock and Tenth Armies, which were in STAVKA reserve, so as to strike harder at the Nazis, stop them and then throw them back from Moscow. Stalin listened attentively to my report, and then asked, 'Are you sure that the enemy has reached a crisis, and that he is not in a position to introduce some large new force into the affair?'

I answered that the enemy was worn out, but that unless fresh forces were brought in the Front's forces would be unable to liquidate his dangerous penetrations. If we did not liquidate these now, the German command would be able to strengthen its forces later on with large reserves, created at the expense of Army Groups North and South, and then our position would become more difficult.

The Supreme Commander said that he would consult the General Staff. On my instruction the Front's Chief of Staff, General Sokolovsky, who also thought it time to bring in the bulk of First Shock and Tenth Armies, telephoned the General Staff and argued the case for handing these armies over to the Western Front as quickly as possible. Late on the evening of 29th November STAVKA's decision was communicated to us; First Shock, Tenth and also all the formations from which Twentieth Army had been formed were subordinated to the Western Front. At the same time we were ordered to present a plan for using them.

Before dawn on 30th November Stalin rang up and asked what the Military Council thought about a counteroffensive by all the Front's forces. I answered that we did not yet have adequate forces or weapons for such a counteroffensive, but that perhaps we could bring one about by development from counterattacks on the wings of the Front.

For the whole of 30th November the Front Command worked on a plan for a counteroffensive using the armies which had been handed over to us. The essence of the decision which we took may be summed up as follows; depending on the time taken to unload and concentrate First Shock, Twentieth and Tenth Armies, the Front would be able to begin the counteroffensive on 3rd or 4th December. The first task would be to defeat the main enemy group on the right wing by attacking towards Klin, Solnechnogorsk and on the Istra axis, and to defeat the Germans on the left wing of the Front by striking at Uzlovaya and Bogoroditsk, into the flank and rear of Guderian's force. The central armies of the Front were to go over to the offensive on 4th or 5th December, with the limited aim of tying down the enemy forces facing them, and making it impossible for him to transfer troops.

Until the counteroffensive began we pursued the aim of stopping the German advance northwest of Moscow and on the Kashira axis, and for this we utilised the forces which were there and, as they arrived, the forward elements of the formations transferred to us from STAVKA reserve.

Our proposal for the counteroffensive, laid out on a map, was reported to STAVKA on 30th November together with an explanatory note, and Stalin confirmed it without alteration. After this the troops were given the following tasks: First Shock Army (Lieutenant-General V I Kuznetsov) to wipe out the enemy forces which had broken through behind the Moscow-Volga canal, then to deploy all its forces in the Dmitrov-Yakhroma area and strike in conjunction with Thirtieth and Twentieth Armies towards Klin, and further in the general direction of Teryayeva Sloboda; Thirtieth Army was given the task of defeating the enemy in the Rogachevo-Borshchevo area and, in co-operation with First Shock Army, of capturing the Reshetnikovo-Klin area, then attacking towards Kostlyakovo and Lotoshino; Twentieth Army was to strike from the Krasnaya Polyana-Bely Rast area, jointly with First Shock and Sixteenth armies, in the general direction of Solnechnogorsk, outflanking it from the south and going further in the general direction of Volokolamsk; besides this, the Sixteenth Army's right wing was to strike towards Kryukovo and on to Istra; Fiftieth Army, on the defensive in the

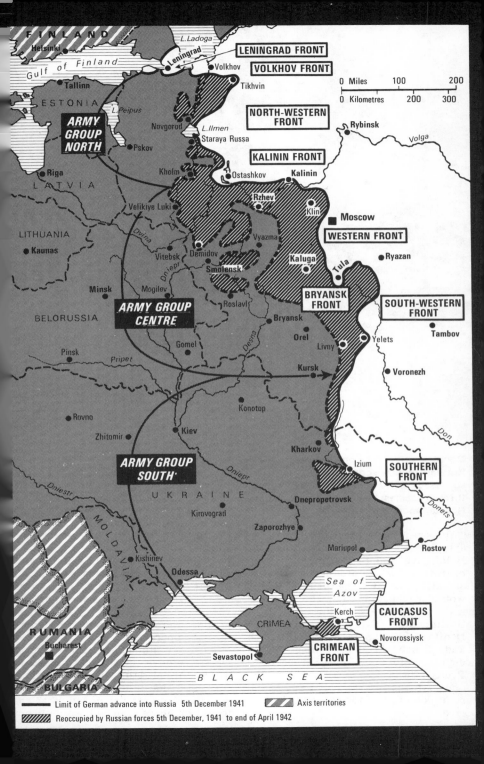

FINLAND

Helsinki

Gulf of Finland

L. Ladoga

Leningrad

Volkhov

LENINGRAD FRONT

VOLKHOV FRONT

Tikhvin

Tallinn

ESTONIA

L. Peipus

Novgorod

L. Ilmen
Staraya Russa

**NORTH-WESTERN
FRONT**

Rybinsk

Volga

Pskov

**ARMY
GROUP
NORTH**

Kholm

Ostashkov

Kalinin

KALININ FRONT

Riga

LATVIA

Dvina

Velikiye Luki

Rzhev

Klin

Moscow

WESTERN FRONT

LITHUANIA

Kaunas

Vitebsk

Demidov

Smolensk

Vyazma

Kaluga

Ryazan

Tula

Dnieper

Minsk

Mogilev

Roslavl

**ARMY GROUP
CENTRE**

Bryansk

**BRYANSK
FRONT**

**SOUTH-WESTERN
FRONT**

BELORUSSIA

Gomel

Desna

Orel

Livny

Yelets

Tambov

Pinsk

Pripet

Kursk

Voronezh

Rovno

Konotop

Don

Zhitomir

Kiev

Kharkov

Izium

**SOUTHERN
FRONT**

**ARMY GROUP
SOUTH·**

Dniepr

UKRAINE

Kirovograd

Dnepropetrovsk

Dniestr

Zaporozhye

Donets

MOLDAVIA

Kishinev

Mariupol

Rostov

Odessa

*Sea of
Azov*

RUMANIA

Bucharest

CRIMEA

Kerch

**CAUCASUS
FRONT**

Novorossiysk

Sevastopol

**CRIMEAN
FRONT**

BULGARIA

B L A C K   S E A

0 Miles 100 200
0 Kilometres 200 300

—— Limit of German advance into Russia 5th December 1941   ▨ Axis territories

▨ Reoccupied by Russian forces 5th December, 1941 to end of April 1942

Dovator's Cossacks on the march.
Russian cavalry scored initial
successes, but failed completely when
thrown recklessly against cool-headed
German machine-gunners

Tula area, was given the task of attacking in the direction of Bolokhovo and Shchekino and then operating in accordance with the situation. Belov's Operational Group would strike out from the Mordves area to Venev and further on to Stalinogorsk (Novomoskovsk), and Dedilovo, in co-operation with Fiftieth and Tenth Armies; Tenth Army, deployed along the lines Serebryanye Prudy-Mikhaylov, was to go into the offensive against Uzlovaya and Bogoroditsk and continue south of the Upa river.

Thus the extra forces of the three armies which had been handed over to us were introduced against the northern and southern groups of Germans.

The four armies of Western Front which were defending in the centre (Fifth, Thirty-third, Forty-third and Forty-ninth) were given the task of pinning down enemy units and formations opposite them by active operations, to prevent him from manoeuvring his forces freely. Since they were very much weakened, these armies were not capable of more decisive operations.

Thus our immediate aim, in short, was to remove the threat to Moscow, and we intended to set the armies their further tasks in accordance with the way the situation developed. With the forces which we then had, we could not

set the troops of the Front more far-reaching and more decisive aims at once. Indeed, despite the transfer to our Front of three armies, we still lacked numerical superiority over the enemy, except in aircraft, and not only that, he even outnumbered us in tanks and artillery. This circumstance was typical of the situation in front of Moscow during that period.

One day when Stalin was talking to me on the telephone (I think it was on the morning of 2nd December, though I do not remember exactly when it was) he asked 'What is the Front's assessment of the enemy and his capabilities?' I replied that the enemy was running out of breath once and for all. It was clear that he was no longer capable of reinforcing his assault groups with reserves, and

without them the German forces would not be able to conduct an offensive. The Supreme Commander said 'Good. I'll ring you again.' I realised that further operations for our forces were under consideration at STAVKA.

About an hour later the Supreme Commander rang up again and asked what the Front intended to do in the next few days. I reported that the troops were preparing for a counter-offensive in accordance with the agreed plan.

During those days STAVKA and the General Staff were thinking how to organise operations by other Fronts (Kalinin Front, and the right wing of Southwestern) so as to give all possible support to the Western Front and achieve a greater effect with

127

Above: Battlefield relic; Russians examine a bowled-over T-38 tank . *Below:*
Tanks were the butter for Zhukov's bread during the Battle of Moscow

Bizarre weapon: the mine dog. Russians trained dogs to run under enemy tanks, laden with explosives. But these two fell to German bullets

the limited forces which we had at our disposal. The Deputy Chief of General Staff, Lieutenant-General AM Vasilevsky, had expounded an idea along these lines in conversations on 1st December on the direct line with the Commander of Kalinin Front, Colonel-General I S Konev. 'To break the German offensive on Moscow.' he said 'and thus not only to save Moscow but to put a start to a serious defeat for the enemy, is possible only by conducting active operations with a decisive objective. If we do not do this in the next few days, it will be too late. Kalinin Front, which occupies an extremely favourable operational position for this objective, cannot be left out of this.'

In a telephone conversation on 2nd December, Stalin said that orders had been given to Kalinin Front and the right wing of Southwestern Front to support our blows, which should be struck simultaneously with the neighbouring Fronts.

Late on the evening of 4th December, the Supreme Commander rang me up on the direct line, and posed the question 'What can we give to help the Front, apart from what has already been given?'

It is quite understandable that taking our extremely limited capabilities at that time into account, we could not ask for much. Therefore above all I thought that we must have support from the air forces of the Supreme Command reserve and the air defence of the homeland. Of course 200 tanks with crews, if not more, were very necessary if we were to develop our offensive quickly, since the Front had very few of them.

'There are no tanks, we can't give you any.' replied Stalin. 'Aircraft there will be. I will ring the General Staff now. Bear in mind that Kalinin Front goes into the offensive on 5th December, and the operational group of the right wing of South-western Front does so from the Yelets area on 6th December.'

Such were all the circumstances which determined the character of Soviet troop operations at the end of November and the beginning of December 1941.

When we were organising the resistance to the enemy in the last days of November and the first days of December, and then began using a more active form – counterattacking – we had no clearly formulated idea in our minds that the counteroffensive which we were devising would be as great as it later turned out. The first tasks for the counteroffensive which we set on 30th November, were in pursuit of an aim which, though important, was still limited – to throw back the enemy forces which threatened most to break through to Moscow. We envisaged that the depth of the strikes would be up to about 37 miles in the north and about one hundred in the south. But it became clear in the course of the counterattacks delivered at the beginning of December, that the enemy was so worn out by the preceding battles, and was so weakened, that he not only could not continue his offensive, but was not in a position to organise a stable defence. And when the Germans began to withdraw on the right and especially on the left wing of our Front, the Front Command began increasing the strength of the blows not only in frontage but also in depth by means of individual orders. and by 5th–6th December, the counter-offensive was already a reality. But as I recall, no special order or general directive for a counteroffensive was ever issued. The combat tasks for the troops, both immediate and longer term, were issued in sequence by separate directives from the Front headquarters.

Thus the counteroffensive in front of Moscow had no sharply defined beginning, as was the case, for example, at Stalingrad. It developed out of counterattacks; air strikes were intensified, additional combined-arms formations were introduced, and so on. It was determined by the entire

course of preceding events; on the one hand the troops of the central axis wore out the enemy, and made him incapable of finishing the operation which he had begun; on the other hand we had collected forces in front of Moscow, and by committing them at the decisive moment we were able first to throw back the most dangerous German groupings and then to set and resolve the task of destroying them.

In those days fierce frosts had settled on the central region of the USSR. The deep snow and the cold seriously hampered troop concentration, regrouping and movement to starting positions. Nevertheless our heroic soldiers and officers of all arms of service overcame the unprecedented difficulties, and were ready at the appointed time to carry out the combat assignments which had been given them.

When we moved from defensive to offensive operations we did not have numerical superiority over the enemy. But our great advantage was the high morale of the Soviet troops, which gave them an influx of energy, and was the result of tremendous Party

Support for the *Wehrmacht*: nose-to-tail road transport, and a Ju-52 supply flight

political work which the officers and political workers carried out on the eve of the counteroffensive at all levels of the Front from Headquarters down to companies and platoons. As a result of it our forces were imbued with confidence in their own forces and in the possibility that the enemy could be beaten in front of Moscow. This turning point, which I would call a psychological one, largely ensured that the truly unprecedented difficulties with which our splendid troops had to contend during the counteroffensive and the general offensive would be overcome. It seems to me that our military historical researchers and writers of memoirs ought to pay more attention to the influence of the psychological factor on the course of combat operations, especially at turning points or at critical moments of a battle or operation. In my view this could bring great benefit.

On 6th December, after concentrated

Russian paratroopers

air strikes and artillery preparation, the troops of the Western Front went over to the counteroffensive north and south of Moscow. A battle developed in which the initiative was entirely in the hands of Soviet troops. By this time formations of Kalinin Front, which had begun its offensive a day earlier, had penetrated the enemy defences south of Kalinin.

On 13th December First Shock Army, together with part of Thirtieth Army, reached Klin. Our troops surrounded the town from all sides then broke in, and after fierce fighting cleared it of Germans on the night of 14th–15th December.

Sixteenth and Twentieth Armies developed their offensive operations successfully. By the evening of 9th December Twentieth Army had reached Solnechnogorsk, while Sixteenth Army liberated Kryukovo on 8th December, then developed its blow towards the Istra reservoir. On 12th December Twentieth Army forced the enemy out of Solnechnogorsk. The advance by Fifth Army's right wing assisted Sixteenth Army's success a great deal. The military operations of Western Front's right wing went on without a pause.

On the left wing, in the Tula area, troops of Fiftieth Army supported a strike by General P A Belov's reinforced cavalry corps, beginning on 3rd December, and jointly set about beating Guderian's Panzer Army. The 3rd and 17th Panzer and 29th Motorised Divisions of this army, began a hasty retreat to Venev leaving about seventy tanks on the battlefield. Our forces were helped to success here by the circumstance that the German Second Panzer Army, in its attempt to outflank Tula from the rear, had become unduly extended and had no reserves left by the time our left flank group attacked. On 6th December our Tenth Army also entered the battle in the Mikhaylov area, where the Germans were trying to hold their defence

Left: **German graves in Klin.** *Above:*
The Russian flag returns to Klin

and cover the flank of Guderian's
retreating Second Panzer Army.

The strike by formations of Fiftieth
Army, which followed from the Tula
area on 8th December, threatened the
retreat routes of the German forces
from Venev and Mikhaylov. Since
Guderian was deeply outflanked and
did not have the forces to parry the
Western Front's blows, and those of
Southwestern Front's operational
group as well, he began hastily to
withdraw his troops in the general
direction of Uzlovaya, Bogoroditsk
and on to Sukhinichi. In their panic
the Germans abandoned their heavy
weapons, vehicles, tractors and tanks
during their retreat. During ten days
of battle troops of the left wing of
Western Front inflicted a severe
defeat on Second Panzer Army and
advanced 81 miles. The troops of
Belov's reinforced Cavalry Corps,

the 112th Tank Division (Colonel A L
Getman) and the Operational Group
of Fiftieth Army (Major-General VS
Popov) particularly distinguished
themselves during the counterstrikes
and the counteroffensive.

Under the blows of the Soviet forces
the enemy began to roll backwards to
the west, and on 12th December the
Military Council of the western Front
reported to the Supreme Commander:
'On 6th December 1941 troops of our
Front, after exhausting the enemy in
the preceding battles, began a decisive
counteroffensive against his flank
strike groups. As a result of the
offensive, both these groups have been
beaten and are withdrawing hastily,
abandoning arms and equipment and
suffering immense casualties.'

The operational concept for further
operations by the Front's forces,
expressed in Command and Staff
directives of the period 13th–24th
December, envisaged a swift advance
by the right wing to the Zubtsov-

Gzhatsk line and by the left to Polotnyany Zavod and Kozelsk; during this the forces of the centre were on the line Mozhaysk-Maloyaroslavets, echelonned backwards. In other words, we intended to create a situation in which our groups which had been advanced on the right and left wings of the Front could create the prerequisites for encircling the main forces of the German Army Group Centre.

I am sometimes asked why the central armies of the Western Front (Thirty-third, Forty-third and Forty-ninth) did not take part in the counterblows and then moved forward only very slowly during the counteroffensive. The fact was that during the defensive battle we had to reinforce the armies of our right and left wings in order to carry out the main task, which was on the flanks of the front. We had to send literally everything possible to the flanks from the central armies, and even after the counteroffensive had begun the armies of the centre were given not one soldier, not one gun, not one machine-gun. They had no capability for any sort of concentrated attacks, so, as we say, they waited for events to develop, and only when the enemy's flanks were beaten in and he began a hasty withdrawal to the Rivers Ruza and Lama, and also to run under blows from Tenth and Fiftieth Armies and Belov's group, did a possibility present itself to move Thirty-third, Forty-third and Forty-ninth Armies at the cost of some regrouping. Their slow and fruitless offensive is explained also by the fact that they had no tanks and inadequate artillery. All the Front's efforts had been applied on the flanks, so that when the main enemy forces had been beaten, the flanks could be pushed forward as quickly as possible and thus place the forces of the enemy's centre under threat.

The air forces of the Front, of the Air Defence Forces and of the Long-Range Air Force, contributed greatly to the success of our December counteroffensive in front of Moscow. The pilots operated self-sacrificingly and skilfully. Thanks to the general efforts of the Front, Long-Range and Air Defence air forces, initiative in the air was wrested from the enemy for the first time since the beginning of the war. The air forces struck systematically at artillery positions, tank units and command posts, and when the Nazi armies began their withdrawal, our aircraft unceasingly assaulted and bombarded the retreating columns of troops. As a result all the roads to the west were cluttered with combat equipment and vehicles which the Germans had abandoned.

As a rule we used our own air forces and those subordinated to us under centralised control, under which approximately three-quarters of it concentrated its efforts on support of our ground operations, striking on the right wing of the Front. The remaining air formations at our disposal, and the three air Divisions allocated from STAVKA Reserve, gave active assistance from the air to Belov's cavalry formations and also to the troops of Fiftieth and Tenth Armies. Air operations were controlled from the command post of the Commander of Air Forces of the Front, Major-General of Aviation S A Khudyakov, alongside my own in Perkhushkovo. Both during the defensive battles and throughout the counteroffensive General Khuyakov was always alongside me. He knew his job excellently, and was able to arrange air operations quickly and precisely wherever and whenever they were needed. The Commander of the Air Operations Groups, Lieutenant-General I F Petrov, and the other air commanders also showed up very well.

Since I have mentioned that both the Staff and the Command Post of the Front were in Perkhushkovo, I would like in passing to answer a question which is sometimes asked of me. 'How do you explain the fact that your Front

How the Russians found them

137

staff and the army staffs were so close to the front line, especially at the end of November and the beginning of December?' All headquarters – of the Front, the armies, divisions and units – were indeed extremely close to the front line at that time, contrary to the accepted standards which envisage taking security measures to protect Commanders and their staffs. But again the explanation lies in the peculiarity and uniqueness of the situation. In this connection I remember an episode which occurred on 2nd December, when there was a breakthrough at the junction of Fifth and Thirty-third Armies. A fairly large enemy group, a reinforced regiment I would say, broke through to the Front Headquarters, and fighting in which the Guard Regiment and staff officers took part broke out in the birch wood where we were located. The Germans were beaten and thrown back. That was the only time this happened, but it does indicate the conditions in which the staff had to work at that time. But all the same, even at the most critical moment of the defensive battle, the thought never entered our heads that we should withdraw the front headquarters further to the rear. Why? Well, because it would at once have become known to the subordinate headquarters and the troops, and what would they have thought of it? 'The Front Command and Staff is making unqualified stern demands that the troops do the impossible, and ordering them to stand till they die, while hundreds and thousands of political workers, propagandists and communists, explain to the troops that behind them is Moscow and there is no room to retreat. Our troops are doing everything within human power, and even more, to fulfil the Motherland's order to stop the enemy then defeat and destroy him. And then, at such a time, the Front headquarters suddenly

Major-General PA Belov watches his cavalrymen file past

Partisans

The lesson of Finland: a Russian ski-patrol, proof that the havoc wrought on the Red Army by Finnish ski-troops during the Winter War had not been in vain

removes and relocates itself!' Of course the front line is not the place for it, but that was how things had to be for the matter in hand, and for firm control of the troops. In this case the normal standards could not be applied.

Besides, the Military Council did not think the main enemy attack would come on that axis, and also bore in mind that communications at Perkhushkovo were excellently organised. I have already had the oppo-

tunity of mentioning this, but would like to touch on it once again, since the given situation applied a well-known stamp to the way in which the troops were controlled.

The nearness of the capital, and use of all lines of the government and civil network of communications, thanks to the indefatigability of the Chief of Communications of the Front, N D Psurtsev, and his sub-ordinates, enabled us to maintain reliable connection by telephone and telegraph channels with STAVKA, the General Staff and all the armies subordinate to the Front, while reserve by-pass communication routes had been made ready in case of emer-

gencies. If necessary the Front staff or command post could be directly connected even with specific divisions.

I must say that the practice of war showed beyond doubt how necessary and useful it was that junior and senior officers should spend time working with their forces before an engagement or battle begins. This must be done so as to help the troops to understand the situation better and to organise the impending operations properly, but when they begin and while they are in progress senior and junior commanders must be at their headquarters or command posts, and direct their troops from there.

These were the ideas by which we were governed in controlling our forces in the Moscow battle. During the period of defensive operations the great extent of the Front (more than 370 miles), the difficulty and great tension of the situation prevented a Front Commander from leaving his headquarters, where all the data on what the enemy was doing, on our own forces, and on the neighbouring Fronts were concentrated in good time, and where constant contact was maintained with STAVKA and the General Staff.

But nevertheless I once had to leave headquarters even during the defensive battle and go to one of the divisions of Sixteenth Army. This is how it happened.

Somehow or other information reached Stalin that our troops had abandoned the town of Dedovsk northwest of Nakhabino. That town was exceedingly close to Moscow, and, naturally, he was very worried by such an unexpected piece of news; for as recently as 28th and 29th November the 9th Guards Rifle Division (Major-General A P Beloborodov) had been successful in repelling repeated fierce enemy attacks in the Istra area. But twenty-four hours had gone by, and it seemed that Dedovsk was in Nazi hands.

Stalin summoned me to the telephone: 'Do you know that Dedovsk has been captured?' 'No, Comrade Stalin, I don't.' The Supreme Commander was not slow to tell me what he thought of my answer, remarking with vexation, 'A Commander must know what is happening on his Front,' and he ordered me to go to the place immediately 'to organise a counterattack personally and get Dedovsk back.' I said that to leave the Front headquarters while the situation was so intense was barely thinkable, and tried to refuse.

'Never mind, we'll manage here somehow; leave Sokolovsky behind instead of you for the time being.'

As soon as I had put down the telephone I contacted General Rokossov-

Inhabitants of Moscow undergoing
military training

sky and demanded that he explain why Front Headquarters had been told nothing about the abandonment of Dedovsk. At once it became clear that the town of Dedovsk had not been captured by the Germans, but that perhaps the village of Dedovo had, as in the Khovanskoye-Dedovo-Snigiri area and southwards of it, the 9th Guards Rifle Division was in heavy fighting preventing an enemy breakthrough along the Volokolamsk highway to Dedovsk and Nakhabino. Clearly there had been a mistake, so I decided to ring STAVKA and explain that it was all a misunderstanding. But there I found I was beating my head against a stone wall. Stalin in the end became angry, insisted on my going to Rokossovsky at once and taking action to recover the wretched village from the enemy beyond doubt, and even ordered me to take the Commander of Fifth Army, General Govorov, with me. 'He is a gunner, let him help Rokossovsky to organise the artillery in the interests of Sixteenth Army.'

There was no point in refusing in such a situation, so I then rang General Govorov and placed the assignment before him. He, entirely reasonably, tried to argue that he saw no necessity for this journey, as Sixteenth Army had its own Head of Artillery, Major-General Kazakov, and, besides, the Army Commander himself knew what to do and how to do it, so why should he, Govorov, leave his own army at such a hot time? To put an end to argument on this question I had to explain to the General that it was an order from Stalin.

We went to Rokossovsky who accompanied us straight away to Beloborodov's division. The divisional commander was not very pleased to see us, as he was then up to the neck in work, and now in addition had to explain about a few houses on the opposite side of a ravine in the village of Dedovo, which the enemy had captured. Beloborodov showed quite convincingly in his report on the situa-

tion that there was no tactical point in recapturing these houses on the other side of a deep ravine, but unfortunately I could not tell him that in this particular case I had to be guided by considerations other than tactical ones. I therefore ordered Beloborodov to send a rifle company with two tanks and throw out the platoon of Germans which had installed itself in the houses, and this was done, I think at dawn on 1st December.

It later turned out that while all this was going on I was being actively sought on every telephone that there was, and since the line of communication between the division and Sixteenth Army had been cut for some time, a signals officer came to Beloborodov's division to tell me. I soon succeeded in establishing contact with General Sokolovsky, who reported that Stalin had already rung the Front headquarters three times to ask 'Where is Zhukov? Why has he gone away?' It appeared that on the morning of 1st December the enemy had begun an offensive on Thirty-third Army's sector, where up to now relative quiet had prevailed.

When Sokolovsky and I had agreed on the steps which must be taken at once to liquidate the new threat, I began trying to contact STAVKA, and succeeded in establishing contact with Vasilevsky, who told me Stalin had ordered me to return at once to the Front headquarters. While I was doing this STAVKA would decide what additional reserves could be given to us to liquidate the enemy breakthrough towards Aprelevka.

When I had returned to the headquarters I at once rang Moscow and this time they connected me with Stalin. I reported that I had acquainted myself with the situation, and told him what steps had been taken or were being taken to wipe out the German units which had broken through in the centre of the Front. Stalin did not return to the conversation about my trip with Govorov to Sixteenth Army, nor about the reason

German unfortunates, thinly-clad, easy targets against the snow.

why he had ordered us to go there. Only at the very end did he ask casually, 'Well, how was Dedovsk?' I replied that the rifle company supported by two tanks which had been sent into the attack had expelled a platoon of Germans from the village of Dedovo. Thus ended one of my trips away from my Front headquarters during the defensive battle in front of Moscow.

But while the counteroffensive was on, visits to the troops had already become a necessity. I had to go to Rokossovsky at Sixteenth Army, Govorov at Fifth Army, Golubev at Forty-third Army, and to Zakharkin at Forty-ninth Army. The main reason why I had to do this was to help the army commanders co-ordinate their activities with their neighbours better, warn them against frontal attacks, make the troops by-pass enemy strongpoints more boldly and pursue him at high speed. I even had to issue a special directive on this, about

a week after the beginning of the counteroffensive. It said in particular: '5. Pursuit is to be conducted at high speed, and the enemy not permitted to break contact. Strong forward detachments are to be widely used to capture road junctions and bottle-necks, to disorganise enemy march and combat columns. 6. I categorically forbid frontal attacks on fortified complexes of enemy resistance. The leading echelons must by-pass them without pausing, leaving the destruction of these complexes to the following echelons.'

Inclusion of these requirements in the directive was determined by experience in the very first days of offensive operations by our forces. The point was that in a number of cases the Armies' assault groups became tied up in prolonged and bloody frontal attacks. In the Klin area, for

The winter gear of the *Wehrmacht*

example, the advance of Thirtieth and First Shock Armies was delayed for this reason. In those days an extraordinary offensive *elan* and an exceedingly high standard of morale were visible everywhere in our forces in those days. Soviet soldiers had at last seen what they had waited for, the Nazi army reeling backwards under their blows. But despite all this, it must not be forgotten that we still lacked adequate experience of fighting, and many of our commanders were unskilful, especially in organising offensive operations. Even though attacking, some of them were not yet fully confident of their forces and occasionally were afraid they themselves would be encircled. And so from time to time units and formations were brought hesitantly into gaps which appeared in the front line. The science of beating a strong and experienced enemy was not easy to

the retreating German forces, and the fight put up by partisan detachments seriously complicated the situation for the Nazis.

You will readily understand that cavalry and skiers could not fully make up for our lack of mobile armoured formations, but all the same they fought heroically and did great damage to the enemy. In the battles on the Klin axis, the cavalrymen of 24th Cavalry Division distinguished themselves, and the men of the I and II Guards Cavalry Corps acquitted themselves outstandingly, but on 19th December near Palashkino village, seven miles northwest of Ruza, the Commander of the II Guards Cavalry Corps, Major-General L M Dovator, and the Commander of 20th Cavalry Division, Lieutenant-Colonel M P Tavliev, were killed during an attack. Their bodies were sent to Moscow for burial, and the Presidium of the Supreme Soviet of the USSR posthumously awarded General Dovator the title of Hero of the Soviet Union.

I must say that during the battle for Leningrad, as at Moscow, Naval Rifle Brigades covered themselves with glory in battle, and made a significant contribution to the general success of the Soviet forces.

As a result of our counteroffensive outside Moscow, the operational-strategic situation on the Western Front on 1st January 1942 was as follows:—

The right wing (First Shock, Twentieth and Sixteenth Armies) was attacking stubbornly against an organised German defence on the line of the Rivers Lama and Ruza (Thirtieth Army, by order of STAVKA, had been handed over to the Kalinin Front);

The centre (Fifth, Thirty-third, Forty-third and Forty-ninth Armies) was developing the offensive from the line of the Rivers Ruza, Nara and Oka towards Mozhaisk, Borovsk, Malo-yaroslavets and Kondrovo, and over-coming enemy opposition.

acquire, and, too, our lack at that time of mobile armoured formations, which could dash swiftly forward into the operational space once they had broken through the defence, was making itself felt acutely.

The Front Command had to send ski, cavalry and airborne units into the rear on to the enemy's withdrawal routes. There too, in the enemy rear, co-ordinating their operations with the Military Councils of the Fronts, Soviet partisans became active against

Another Russian assault-wave moves up

The left wing (Fiftieth and Tenth Armies and General Belov's group) was successfully developing pursuit of the enemy in the general directions of Yukhnov, Mosalsk and Kirov.

By this time troops of Kalinin Front were striking in the general direction of Staritsa-Rzhev, while the left wing of this Front, co-operating as before with the right wing of the Western Front, was fighting on the line of the River Lama where the Germans were putting up stubborn resistance. The troops of the newly formed Bryansk Front were fighting on the line of the Oka, lagging some distance behind the left wing of the Western Front.

In these circumstances the armies of the Western Front's left wing, which had penetrated deeply into the Nazi positions and thus were capable of developing the offensive successfully, were best placed to undertake it. But to develop the offensive fresh forces were necessary, and by that time the Front no longer had any reserves. We asked STAVKA for reserves but were refused.

In the first days of January, when our troops reached the line running from Oreshki via Staritsa, the Lama and Ruza rivers, Maloyaroslavets, Tikhonova Pustyn, Kaluga, Mosalsk, Kirov, Sukhinichi, Belev and Mtsensk to Novosil, we judged that the first stage of our counteroffensive was basically at an end. We thought that as far as the Fronts of the Western axis (Western, Kalinin and Bryansk) were concerned the subsequent stage should consist of continuing the offensive, after reinforcement with the appropriate troops and material, until it was fully completed; that is, until we had restored the positions occupied by those Fronts before the Germans had begun the offensive operations codenamed 'Typhoon'. If we had succeeded in getting from STAVKA just four armies of reinforcements (one each for Kalinin and Bryansk Fronts, and two for the Western Front) we would have had a real chance of inflicting further defeats

on the Germans, pushing them back even further from Moscow, and reaching the Vitebsk-Smolensk-Bryansk line. In any case, there was no disagreement among either the members of the Military Council or of the Front Headquarters that in continuing the counteroffensive so as to inflict the most damage on the Germans all available forces must be used on the Western strategic axis. I think this attitude correctly reflected the situation which existed at the Front.

There is no doubt that the December counteroffensive on the central strategic axis had been very successful. The assault groups of Army Group Centre had suffered a severe defeat and had retreated. But as a whole the enemy was still strong not only on the western axis but on the others as well. On the central sector of the Front, he was putting up a fierce resistance and Soviet offensives in South and North, at Rostov and Tikhvin, which began successfully, did not reach a fitting conclusion, but became long-drawn out. But Stalin was influenced by the successes which we had achieved in the course of the counteroffensive, and inclined to optimism. He thought that the Germans, who had not been prepared for fighting in winter, would be no more able to withstand the Red Army's attacks on the other sectors of the Front. That sparked the idea in his mind of an offensive on the entire Front from Lake Ladoga to the Black Sea, to be begun as soon as possible.

Both I and the Member of the Military Council of the Front, N A Bulganin, were frequently at STAVKA in those days, as Stalin summoned us many times, explaining that he wanted to consult us personally about the state of affairs on the Front and our estimate of the situation for the immediate future.

On the morning of 5th January 1942, I was summoned to Moscow in my capacity as a Member of STAVKA to consider the plan for further operations. The members of the State Defence Committee, the Chief of the General Staff, VM Shaposhnikov, and if my memory does not betray me, his deputy AN Vasilevsky, were present at that session, and NA Voznesensky (in charge of war production) was also invited. Shaposhnikov gave a short account of the situation at the Fronts and notes on the plan for our operations. It emerged that while the counteroffensive by the Fronts of the Western axis went on, Stalin intended to put the Soviet forces on all the other axes as well on to the offensive, with the object of defeating the Germans in front of Leningrad, west of Moscow and in the south of the country. Thus the counteroffensive on the central axis was meant to grow into a general offensive along the entire Front.

The main blow was to be struck at Army Group Centre, which was to be smashed by the forces of the Western, Kalinin, the left wing of Northwestern and Bryansk Fronts. Army Group North was to be defeated and an end put to the blockade of Leningrad, by Leningrad Front, the right wing of Northwestern Front and the Baltic fleet, while the Southwestern and Southern Fronts were to defeat Army Group South and liberate the Donbass. Caucasus Front and the Black Sea Fleet were expected to liberate the Crimea. The general offensive was to begin very soon.

Summing up Shaposhnikov's statement, Stalin said, 'The Germans are in despair at present, because they were beaten in front of Moscow, and had prepared badly for the winter. Now is the most suitable moment for going over to a general offensive.'

The plan for a general offensive was a very big one, but we had at that time neither the troops nor the resources to execute it.

'Who wants to comment?' asked Stalin, after the Chief of the General Staff had expounded the whole of this plan. I asked for the floor and said that the Fronts must continue the offensive on the Western strategic axis, where the most favourable conditions had been created for it and where the enemy had not yet been able to restore the fighting ability of his units. But to do this they must be made up to strength in manpower and equipment, and reinforced with reserves, above all armoured units, without which it would be difficult to carry out the assignments planned for them. As for an offensive by our forces at Leningrad and on the southwestern axis, they were faced there with the need to break through strong defensive positions. Without powerful artillery resources they would be unable to do so, but would merely be worn down, with heavy and completely unjustified casualties. Therefore the Fronts of the western axis must be strengthened and it was here that the most powerful offensive should be waged, while on the other axes we should for the time being give up the idea of an offensive.

I understood from Stalin's interjections while I was speaking that the decision had already been taken and would not be re-examined. However, Voznesensky, who spoke immediately after me, also came out against the general offensive, arguing that we did not have sufficient material resources to supply simultaneous offensives by all Fronts. Stalin allowed him to finish and then said: 'I have spoken to Timoshenko (C-in-C in the South), he is in favour of attacking. We must chew up the Germans as quickly as possible, so that they won't be able to attack in the spring.'

Malenkov and Beria supported Stalin, saying that Voznesensky always found unforeseen difficulties, and that these could be overcome. Nobody else wanted to express an opinion, so the Supreme Commander ended the discussion with the words, 'On that, I think we will stop the talking.'

I formed the impression that Stalin had summoned the military to the STAVKA, not to discuss the sense of

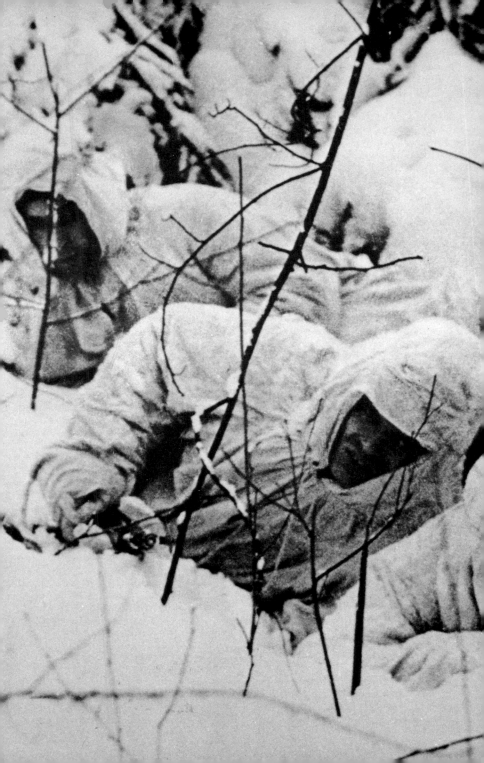

mounting a general-offensive, but in order to 'give the soldiers a push', as he was sometimes fond of saying. When we had left his office Shaposhnikov said, 'You were wasting your time arguing. This question was decided in advance by the Supremo. The directives for almost all the Fronts have already been sent out, and they will begin the offensive in a few days' time.'

'Then why did he ask for opinions?'

'I don't know, my dear fellow, I don't know,' answered Shaposhnikov and sighed heavily.

From what he had said and the phrases which I have quoted above, it became clear to me that the plan for a general offensive had not originated in the General Staff.

The winter offensive operations by Leningrad, Volkhov, and Northwestern Front ended far short of their objectives, as everyone knows. The basic reason for this also lies in the lack of manpower and material necessary to break the enemy resistance. The offensive mounted by Southern and Southwestern Fronts also began to die out quickly, since they had no superiority in men or material, and met with stubborn opposition.

What I am now saying underlines the chances which we missed and concerns the field of strategic planning and use of reserves. However, none of this can denigrate in any way from the importance of the victory which the Soviet forces won in the battle of Moscow. The Nazis lost on the fields of Moscow area altogether more than 500,000 men, 1,300 tanks, 2,500 guns, more than 15,000 vehicles and much other equipment, while the Germans were thrown back from Moscow, 95 to 190 miles to the west.

In his description of the Moscow battle General Westphal had to admit that 'the German army which previously had been considered invincible, was on the verge of annihilation'.

Russian scouts on patrol near German front line

Anti-tank guns near Moscow

Other generals of the Nazi army, such as Tippelskirch, Blumentritt, Manteuffel and many others make the same admission.

The counteroffensive of 1941–42 took place in the difficult conditions of a snowy and severe winter and, most important of all, without numerical superiority over the enemy. We had more Armies than the enemy did, but each barely equalled a German Army Corps in manpower and weaponry, while on top of this the Front had no large armoured or motorised infantry formations at its disposal. Modern offensive operations of decisive aim and large scope cannot be conducted without them, as experience of war has shown. Only when powerful armour and motorised infantry formations are available can one pre-empt the enemy in manoeuvre, get round his flanks quickly, emerge on his rear lines of communications, surround and cut up his forces.

I am often asked 'Where was Stalin during the battle of Moscow?' Stalin was in Moscow, organising manpower and resources to defeat the enemy in front of Moscow. We must give him his due. With the support of the State Defence Committee, the members of STAVKA and the creative team of senior members of the People's Commissariats, he accomplished a great work in organising the strategic reserves and materials – technical resources necessary for armed conflict. One might say that he achieved what was almost impossible by his stern exactingness. During the battle of Moscow he was very attentive to advice, but unfortunately he occasionally took decisions which did not meet the real situation, as with his withdrawal of First Shock Army into reserve and his development of an offensive by all Fronts.

In the battle of Moscow the Red Army inflicted a very great strategic defeat on the main group of German forces, for the first time in six months of war. There had been relatively successful operations by Soviet troops

For thousands of Germans the end of it all: surrender in the snow

on some other sectors of the Soviet-German Front before the fighting in the Moscow area, but none of them could be compared in magnitude with the results of the great battle in front of Moscow, where a well-organised and solid defence against superior Nazi forces, and a quick transition to the counteroffensive enriched Soviet military art, and showed the growing operational and tactical maturity of Soviet military leaders.

In the fierce and bloody battle for Moscow all our sub-units and formations showed extreme steadfastness and doggedness. Soviet soldiers, from private to general, carried out their sacred duty to the Motherland with honour, displayed mass heroism, spared neither strength nor life itself to defend Moscow. Alongside them were our splendid partisans, men and women, and the workers gave invaluable assistance to the troops. Great also was the service of our Communist Party, in that it succeeded in mobilising the incalculable national strength and inspired the Soviet people to gain victory.

When I am asked what I remember most of all from the late war, I always answer 'The battle for Moscow'. A quarter of a century has gone past, but these historical events and battles have remained in my memory until now. In severe, sometimes catastrophically difficult and complicated conditions, our troops were hardened, made braver, accumulated experience, and when the necessary minimum of technical resources had been delivered into their hands, they turned from a retreating and defending force into a powerful offensive one. A grateful posterity will never forget those hard and heroic days for the Soviet people, nor the military achievements of the soldiers in the Soviet armed forces. In the battle for Moscow was laid a firm foundation for the subsequent defeat of Nazi Germany.

Bibliography

The Red Army before Barbarossa; History of the Second World War volume 2
Malcolm Mackintosh (Purnell, London)
The Wehrmacht before Barbarossa; History of the Second World War volume 2
John Erickson (Purnell, London)
Battle for Moscow: the German View; History of the Second World War volume 2
Generalmajor (AD) Alfred Philippi (Purnell, London)
Battle for Moscow: the Russian View; History of the Second World War volume 2
Colonel D M Proektor (Purnell, London)
The Russian Recovery: History of the Second World War volume 2
John Erickson (Purnell, London)
Kiew. Die Grösste Kesselschlacht der Geschichte: W Haupt (Podzun Verlag, Germany)
V Nachale Voyny Marshal A I Yeremenko (Moscow)
Besprimerny Podvig Marshals Zhukov, Koner, Sokolovsky, Yeremenko et al (Moscow)
Inside Hitler's Headquarters 1939–1945 General W Warlimont (Weidenfeld & Nicolson, London. Praeger, New York)
Russia at War 1941–1945 Alexander Werth (Pan, London. Dutton, New York)
Barbarossa Alan Clark (Hutchinson, London. New American Library, New York)